pianists for the connoisseur

michelangeli
cortot
weissenberg
curzon
solomon
ney

in memory of susan ann hunt
19 march 1912 - 10 january 2002

discographies
compiled by
john hunt

contents

Pianists For The Connoisseur
Published by John Hunt.
Designed by Richard Chluparty
Drawings by Brian Pinder
© 2002 John Hunt
reprinted 2009
ISBN 978-1-901395-12-9

acknowledgement

these publications have been made possible by contributions or advance subscriptions from the following

Stefano Angeloni	Stathis Arfanis
Yoshihiro Asada	Derek Bevan
E.C. Blake	Gordon Buffard
Edward Chibas*	Robert Dandois
Dennis Davis	F. De Vilder
Richard Dennis	John Derry
Hans-Peter Ebner*	Henry Fogel*
T.J. Foley	Nobuo Fukumoto
Peter Fülop	Carlos Ginebrada
Philip Goodman	Jean-Pierre Goossens
Johann Gratz	Michael Harris*
Tadashi Hasegawa*	Naoya Hirabayashi
Andrew Keener	Rodney Kempster
Detlef Kissmann	John Larsen
Elisabeth Legge-Schwarzkopf	Douglas MacIntosh
John Mallinson*	Carlo Marinelli
Philip Moores	Bruce Morrison
W. Moyle	Alessandro Nava
Alan Newcombe	Hugh Palmer*
Jim Parsons*	Laurence Pateman
David Patmore*	James Pearson
Tully Potter	Patrick Russell
Ingo Schwarz	Robin Scott
Tom Scragg*	Graham Silcock
Yoshihiko Suzuki*	Michael Tanner
Julian Tremayne	Urs Weber*
Graeme Wright*	Stephen Wright
Ken Wyman	Ferenc Zemplenyi
Koji Kinoshita	

*indicates life subscriber

Pianists for the connoisseur

The title of this collection of pianist discographies evokes names which perhaps today shine less brightly in the gallery of "collectables" than those of Horowitz, Rubinstein, Arrau or Schnabel. The reasons for this are manifold: imposed or voluntary retirement from the concert platform at a comparatively early age may account for a less starry image in the eyes of the record-buying public (Solomon and Weissenberg could come in this category); eccentric or hypercritical behaviour resulting in a limited performing repertoire (Michelangeli and Curzon).

Alfred Cortot was a poet of the keyboard rather than a virtuoso, and yet was obviously at home in the recording studio, seeking perfection in endless takes of the same work, many of which were never approved for issue (especially those of his last years). And like Cortot, Elly Ney's heyday was in that seemingly remote pre-war period before she became embroiled in her country's dark political fate, and the resulting failure ever to become fully rehabilitated as far as her artistic reputation was concerned.

LA VOCE
DEL PADRONE

SUPPLEMENTO DISCHI

A. BENEDETTI MICHELANGELI

As usual I have striven to include as many catalogue numbers as possible in the various formats of 78, 45, lp, cd, vhs video, dvd video and dvd audio, but am happy and grateful to hear from readers who can point out omissions. Japanese issue numbers are only included where these were first or only publications (as is the case with some Cortot material).

Recording dates are given, where known, in the first column of the layout; orchestras, conductors and other soloists where applicable in the second column. Forward slash in the title heading for a work indicates that the information after the slash is the larger work from which the particular section or movement is taken.

My gratitude goes to those who have assisted with information and other input to these discographies: Francoise Bickert (Colosseum Records), Richard Chlupaty, Siam Chowkwanyun, Brian Crimp, Michael Gray, Syd Gray, Bill Holland, Ken Jagger, Floris Juynboll, Roderick Krüsemann, Alan Newcombe, Luis Luna, Brian Pinder, Tully Potter and Malcolm Walker.

John Hunt copyright 2002

arturo benedetti michelangeli

1925-1995

Arturo Benedetti Michelangeli

drawing by brian pinder

ISAAC ALBENIZ (1860-1909)

malaguena/recuerdos de viaje
milan
1942

78: hmv (italy) DA 5432
45: hmv (italy) 7EQ 3123/7EQ 3170/
    ERQ 245
lp: hmv (italy) QALP 10341
lp: emi 3C053 17017/3C153 50104-50106/
    3C163 50104-50106
lp: melodiya D 30749-30750
cd: emi CDH 763 4902
cd: warner fonit 3984 269022
cd: piano library PL 252-255
cd: arkadia CDHP 624/78563
cd: notablu 935 1103-1104
cd: hommage 700 1860/700 1850
cd: hall of fame 220017

JOHANN SEBASTIAN BACH (1685-1750)

italian concerto

milan
22 january
1943

78: telefunken SKB 3320-3321
lp: rococo 2125
cd: teldec 0630 133032/4509 936712
cd: piano library PL 183/PL 252-255
cd: classico PTC 2005
cd: pearl GEMMCDS 9086
cd: magic talent CD 48071
cd: arkadia CDHP 624/78563
cd: hommage 700 1855/700 1850
cd: hall of fame 220017

chaconne from partita no 2 bwv 1004, arranged by busoni

london
27 october
1948

78: hmv DB 21005-21006
lp: hmv (italy) QALP 5345/QBLP 1044
lp: emi 3C053 00656/3C153 50104-50106/
 3C163 50104-50106
cd: emi CDH 764 4902/CDH 769 2412/
 CDE 575 2302
cd: arkadia 78563
cd: notablu 935 1091-1092
cd: hall of fame 220017

warsaw
13 march
1955

lp: muza SX 1900
lp: rococo 2122
lp: cetra LO 525
lp: paragon LBI 53010/1001-1003
lp: discoreale 10072-10074
cd: melodram MEL 28019
cd: polskie nagrania PNCD 328

lugano
21 may
1973

lp: rococo 2069
lp: discocorp RR 404
cd: music and arts CD 817

bregenz
15 january
1988

cd: aura AUR 2062
issued by aura as a single cd or in an unnumbered set

LUDWIG VAN BEETHOVEN (1770-1827)

piano concerto no 1

vienna	vienna	lp: dg 2531 302
21 september	symphony	cd: dg 419 2482/447 6432/449 7572
1979	giulini	*also unpublished video recording; unofficial lp*
		edition also issued by rococo

piano concerto no 3

vienna	vienna	cd: dg 423 2302/447 6432/449 7572
1 february	symphony	*also unpublished video recording*
1979	giulini	

piano concerto no 4

belgrade	belgrade	lp: rococo 2113
7 october	symphony	lp: discocorp IGI 359
1973	zdravkovic	cd: legends LGD 100
		cd: exclusive EX91T 17
		according to andrew f.wilson (international piano
		quarterly summer 2001) the soloist in this
		recording is not michelangeli, although he did
		perform the concerto in belgrade on that date

beethoven **piano concerto no 5 "emperor"**

geneva	suisse romande	cd: musica helvetica SE 2/MHCD 73.5
11 november	orchestra	cd: eremitage ERM 183
1942	ansermet	cd: piano library PL 252-255
		cd: warner fonit 3984 269022
		cd: magic talent CD 48071
		cd: hommage 100 1855/100 1850
		also published by aura in an unnumbered
		cd set; some editions are dated 8 july 1939;
		all editions comprise only a 2'16" fragment
		from the opening movement (bulk of the
		recording presumably lost)
turin	rai torino	lp: replica RPL 2457-2459
24 november	orchestra	cd: arkadia CD 609/CDHP 609
1947	rossi	cd: warner 0927 406482
prague	prague symphony	cd: praga PR 250.021/PR 256.003
29 may	smetacek	
1957		
vatican city	rai roma	cd: memoria ABM 999.001
27-28	orchestra	*according to harry chin and carlo palese*
april	freccia	*the conductor of this recording was*
1960		*fernando previtali*
rome	rai roma	lp: cetra LAR 44
14 may	orchestra	lp: cls records RPCL 2003
1960	freccia	cd: cetra CDAR 2006
		cd: arkadia CD 505/CDHP 505
		cd: green line 3CLC 4005
		cd: bella musica CD 31600
		cd: virtuoso 269.7082
		cd: notablu 935.1091-1092
		cd: galileo GL 5
		cd: hommage 700 1855/700 1850

beethoven piano concerto no 5/concluded

new york	new york	lp: discocorp IGI 359
8 january	philharmonic	cd: nuova cra 013.6331
1966	steinberg	cd: memories HR 4368-4369

bergamo	rai milano	lp: discocorp IGI 327
22 june	orchestra	
1966	caracciolo	

helsinki	swedish radio	lp: rococo 2047
20 may	orchestra	cd: legends LGD 115
1969	celibidache	cd: as-disc AS 320
		cd: arkadia CD 592/CDHP 592/LE 951
		cd: notes PGP 11002

paris	orchestre	lp: rococo 2126
16 october	national	lp: baton 1010
1974	celibidache	lp: electrocord ECE 02600
		' cd: arkadia CD 609/CDHP 609
		cd: music and arts CD 296/CD 4296
		cd: arlecchino ARLA 06
		cd: live classics best (japan) LCB 115
		music and arts incorrectly dated 1975 and
		incorrectly describes orchestra as paris symphony

vienna	vienna	lp: dg 2531 385
1 february	symphony	cd: dg 419 2492/447 6432
1979	giulini	*also unpublished video recording*

the japanese cd label galileo (GL 5) has also issued an undated performance of the concerto by michelangeli and the munich philharmonic orchestra conducted by daniel barenboim but concert listings available do not confirm that this performance took place beethoven **piano sonata no 3 op 2 no 3**

milan	78: hmv (italy) DB 5442-5444
1941	lp: hmv (italy) QALP 10408
	cd: emi CDH 764 4902
	cd: piano library PL 252-255
	cd: notablu 935 1103-1104
	cd: warner fonit 3984 269012
	cd: hommage 700 1858/700 1850
	cd: arkadia 78563
	cd: hall of fame 220017

buenos aires	cd: aura AUR 2172
21 july	*issued by aura as a single cd or in an unnumbered set*
1949	

arezzo	lp: cetra LO 517/DOC 46
12 february	lp: cls records RPCL 2005
1952	cd: arkadia CD 903/CDGI 903
	cd: archipel ARPCD 0054

warsaw	lp: rococo 2122
13 march	lp: cetra LO 525
1955	lp: muza SX 1898
	lp: discoreale 10072-10074
	lp: paragon DSV 1001-1003
	lp: grandi concerti GCL 49
	cd: melodram MEL 28019
	cd: polskie nagrania PNCD 351
	cd: classico PCT 2018

toronto	vhs video: video artists international
24 february	VAIA 69435
1970	dvd video: video artists international
	VAIDVD 4213
	vhs video edition incorrectly dated 2 november
	1970, presumably the date on which the tv
	recording was originally screened

beethoven piano sonata no 3/concluded

turin	lp: rococo 2161
december	lp: oversea 20013
1962	lp: maison blanche MBL 1005.10
	cd: eremitage ERM 123/ERM 302
	vhs video: rai VRN 2129

new york	cd: legends LGD 120
21 january	cd: notes PGP 11012
1966	cd: as-disc AS 330

vatican city	cd: memoria ABM 999.001
13 june	cd: aura AUR 2022
1987	*issued by aura as single cd or in an unnumbered set*

piano sonata no 4 op 7

bonn	lp: rococo 2069
6 may	
1970	

munich	lp: dg 2530 197/2543 505/419 2481
august	cd: dg 419 2482/447 6432/457 7622
1971	cd: philips 456 9042

london	cd: bbc legends BBCL 40642
13 april	
1982	

piano sonata no 11 op 22

paris	cd: exclusive EX92T 14
11 november	cd: music and arts CD 1036
1978	cd: live classics best (japan) LCB 115

lugano	cd: aura AUR 2232
4 april	
1981	

beethoven **piano sonata no 12 op 26 "funeral march"**

bern	lp: rococo 2117
18 march	lp: music masters MJA 100
1975	lp: discocorp IGI 334
lugano	cd: aura AUR 2232
4 april	
1981	
london	cd: exclusive EX92T 14
13 april	cd: music and arts CD 1036
1982	cd: live classics best (japan) LCB 121
	cd: bbc legends BBCL 40642

beethoven **piano sonata no 32 op 111**

london
14 may
1961

lp: grandi concerti GCL 49
cd: notes PGP 11012
cd: legends LGD 120
cd: as-disc AS 330
cd: memories HR 4368-4369
cd editions are incorrectly dated october 1961

rome
4 march
1965

lp: decca LXT 6181/SXL 6181/414 0651
lp: london (usa) CM 9446/CS 6446
lp: telefunken SMD 1199/641 302/
    641 551AN
cd: decca 417 7722
private recording arranged by michelangeli

bonn
6 may
1970

lp: rococo 2096
cd: private issue vienna

bregenz
15 january
1988

cd: aura AUR 2082
issued by aura as single cd or in an unnumbered set

london
10 may
1990

cd: eremitage ERM 432
also issued by aura in an unnumbered cd set

JOHANNES BRAHMS (1833-1897)

four balladen op 10

london 18 march 1973	unpublished private recording
lugano 21 may 1973	lp: rococo 2064 lp: discocorp RR 404 cd: music and arts CD 817
vatican city 29 april 1977	cd: aura AUR 2122 *issued by aura as single cd or in an unnumbered set*
paris 11 november 1978	cd: ams AMS 042-043
hamburg february 1981	lp: dg 2531 017 cd: dg 400 0432/447 6432/457 7622 cd: philips 456 9042
lugano 7 april 1981	cd: aura AUR 2192 *issued by aura as single cd or in an unnumbered set*

brahms **variations on a theme of paganini**

london
26 october
1948
	78: hmv DB 6909-6910
	lp: hmv (italy) QALP 5345/QBLP 1044
	lp: emi 3C053 00656/3C153 50104-50106/
	  3C163 50104-501106/100 6561
	lp: melodiya D 26603-26604
	cd: emi CDH 764 4902/CDH 769 2412/
	  ÇDE 575 2302
	cd: notablu 935.1103-1104
	cd: philips 456 9042
	cd: hall of fame 220017

arezzo 12 february 1952	lp: cetra LO 517/DOC 46 lp: cls records RPCL 2005 cd: arkadia CD 903/CDGI 903 cd: archipel ARPCD 0054
warsaw 13 march 1955	lp: rococo 2122 lp: cetra LO 525 lp: muza SX 1900 cd: melodram MEL 28019 cd: classico PTC 2018 cd: polskie nagrania PNCD 328
london 18 march 1973	unpublished private recording *recording incomplete*
lugano 21 may 1973	lp: rococo 2069 lp: discocorp RR 404 cd: music and arts CD 817
bregenz 15 january 1988	cd: aura AUR 2062 *issued by aura as single cd or in an unnumbered set*

FREDERIC CHOPIN (1810-1849)

piano sonata no 2 "funeral march"

arezzo	lp: cetra LO 517/DOC 46
12 february	lp: paragon LBI 53009/DSV 1001-1003
1952	lp: discoreale 10072-10073
	lp: melodiya M10 44853 000
	lp: grandi concerti GCL 11
	cd: arkadia CD 903/CDGI 903
	cd: archipel ARPCD 0054

london	lp: rococo 2088
30 june	lp: discocorp R 2088
1959	lp: cls records RPCL 2004
	cd: music and arts CD 955/CD 4955
	cd: bramante BLICD 7004

prague	cd: praga PR 250 042/PR 256 003
3 june	
1960	

turin	lp: music masters MJA 100
december	vhs video: rai VRN 2131
1962	

brescia	cd: foné 90F 32
23 june	*dated by foné as 17 june 1967*
1967	

tokyo	cd: music and arts CD 1036
29 october	cd: legends LGD 100
1973	cd: exclusive EX92T 14

vatican city	cd: aura AUR 2122
29 april	*issued by aura as single cd or in an unnumbered set*
1977	

further performance of the sonata issued on cd by aura (AUR 2212) dated 4 june 1968, although concert cannot be traced as having taken place on that date chopin **andante spianato et grande polonaise**

buenos aires	cd: aura AUR 2172
21 july	*issued by aura as single cd and in an unnumbered set*
1949	

turin	lp: rococo 2128
december	lp: discoreale 10072-10074
1962	lp: paragon LBI 53009/DSV 1001-1003
	lp: discocorp IGI 350
	lp: oversea 20015
	lp: maison blanche MBL 1005.10
	cd: cetra CDE 1021
	cd: eremitage ERM 122/ERM 301
	cd: music and arts CD 924
	vhs video: rai VRN 2131

brescia	cd: foné 90F 32
23 june	cd: aura AUR 2082
1967	*issued by aura as single cd or in an unnumbered set;*
	dated by foné as 17 june 1967

bregenz	cd: aura AUR 2112
20 march	*issued by aura as single cd and in an unnumbered set;*
1985	*dated by aura as 3 march 1985*

vatican city	cd: aura AUR 2042
13 june	cd: memoria ABM 999.001
1987	*issued by aura as single cd and in an unnumbered set*

london	cd: eremitage ERM 432
10 may	*also issued by aura in an unnumbered set*
1990	

further performance of the piece issued on cd by aura (AUR 2212) dated 7 march 1985,
although concert cannot be traced as having taken place on that date

chopin **ballade no 1 in g minor**

london 4 march 1957	cd: testament SBT 2088

prague
30 may
1957

cd: praga PR 250 042

turin
december
1962

lp: discocorp IGI 350
lp: oversea 20015
lp: maison blanche MBL 1005.10
cd: cetra CDE 1021/CDAR 2002/AR 01
cd: music and arts CD 924
cd: eremitage ERM 122/ERM 302
cd: hommage 700 1859/700 1850
cd: warner fonit 0927 406472
vhs video: rai VRN 2131
hommage and warner fonit editions dated 1963

brescia
23 june
1967

cd: foné 90F 32
cd: aura AUR 2082
issued by aura as single cd and in an unnumbered set;
foné dated 17 june 1967

munich
october
1971

lp: dg 2530 236
lp: melodiya C10 19099-19100
cd: dg 413 4492/447 6432

bregenz
20 march
1985

cd: aura AUR 2112
issued by aura as single cd or in an unnumbered set;
dated by aura as 3 march 1985

chopin **berceuse in d flat**

milan	78: telefunken SKB 3289
9 september	cd: teldec 4509 936712/0630 133032
1942	cd: piano library PL 183/PL 252-255
	cd: classico PTC 2005
	cd: pearl GEMMCDS 9086
	cd: arkadia CD 624/CDHP 624
	cd: magic talent CD 48071
	cd: hommage 700 1859/700 1850
	cd: hall of fame 220017
turin	lp: rococo 2128
december	lp: discocorp IGI 350
1962	lp: oversea 20111
	lp: maison blanche MBL 1005.10
	cd: eremitage ERM 122/ERM 301
	cd: music and arts CD 924
	cd: aura AUR 2042
	vhs video: rai VRN 2131
	issued by aura as single cd and in unnumbered set

chopin **fantasy in f minor**
london   cd: testament SBT 2088
4 march
1957

turin   lp: rococo 2128
december   lp: discocorp IGI 350
1962   lp: oversea 20111
                                                lp: maison blanche MBL 1005.10
                                                cd: cetra CDE 1042/CDAR 2002/AR 1
                                                cd: eremitage ERM 123/ERM 301
                                                cd: history 20.3169.306
                                                cd: music and arts CD 924
                                                cd: hommage 700 1860/700 1850
                                                cd: warner fonit 0927 406472
                                                 vhs video: rai VRN 2130
                                                hommage and warner fonit editions dated 1963

bregenz   cd: aura AUR 2112/AUR 2272
20 march   *AUR 2112 is dated 3 march 1985 and is issued*
1985   *as single cd and in an unnumbered set*

mazurka in b minor op 30 no 2
munich   lp: dg 2530 236
october   lp: melodiya C10 19099-19100
1971   cd: dg 413 4492/447 6432
                                                cd: philips 456 9042

chopin **mazurka in d flat op 30 no 3**

turin	lp: rococo 2128
december	lp: discocorp IGI 350
1962	lp: oversea 20111
	lp: maison blanche MBL 1005.10
	cd: cetra CDE 1042/CDAR 2002/AR 1
	cd: eremitage ERM 122/ERM 301
	cd: music and arts CD 924
	cd: aura AUR 2042
	cd: hommage 700 1859/700 1850
	cd: warner fonit 0927 406472
	vhs video: rai VRN 2131
	aura edition is issued as single cd or in an
	unnumbered set; hommage and warner fonit
	editions are dated 1963

brescia	cd: foné 90F 32
23 june	cd: aura AUR 2082
1967	*foné edition is dated 17 june 1967; aura edition*
	is issued as single cd or in an unnumbered set

munich	lp: dg 2530 236
october	lp: melodiya C10 19099-19100
1971	cd: dg 413 4492/447 6432
	cd: philips 456 9042

mazurka in g sharp minor op 33 no 1

brescia	cd: foné 90F 32
23 june	*incorrectly dated 17 june 1967*
1967	

munich	lp: dg 2530 236
october	lp: melodiya C10 19099-19100
1971	cd: dg 413 4492/447 6432
	cd: philips 456 9042

mazurka in c op 33 no 3

brescia	cd: aura AUR 2082
23 june	*issued as single cd and in an unnumbered set*
1967	

chopin **mazurka in b minor op 33 no 4**

milan	78: telefunken SKB 3289
9 september	cd: teldec 4509 936712/0630 133032
1942	cd: piano library PL 183/PL 252-255
	cd: pearl GEMMCDS 9086
	cd: classico PTC 2005
	cd: arkadia CDHP 624
	cd: history 20.3169.306
	cd: magic talent CD 48071
	cd: hommage 700 1859/700 1850
	cd: hall of fame 220017

buenos aires	cd: aura AUR 2172
21 july	*issued as a single cd and in an unnumbered set*
1949	

turin	lp: rococo 2128
december	lp: discocorp IGI 350
1962	lp: oversea 20111
	lp: maison blanche MBL 1005.10
	cd: cetra CDE 1042/CDAR 2002/AR 1
	cd: eremitage ERM 122/ERM 301
	cd: music and arts CD 924
	cd: hommage 700 1859/700 1850
	cd: aura AUR 2042
	cd: warner fonit 0927 406472
	vhs video: rai VRN 2131
	aura edition is issued as a single cd and in an
	unnumbered set; hommage and warner fonit
	editions are dated 1963

brescia	cd: aura AUR 2112
23 june	*dated 17 june 1967; issued as a single cd and*
1967	*in an unnumbered set*

chopin mazurka op 33 no 4/concluded

munich	lp: dg 2530 236
october	lp: melodiya C10 19099-19100
1971	cd: dg 413 4492/447 6432
	cd: philips 456 9042

bregenz	cd: aura AUR 2112
20 march	*dated 3 march 1985; issued as a single cd and*
1985	*in an unnumbered set*

london	cd: eremitage ERM 432
10 may	*also issued by aura in an unnumbered set*
1990	

a version of the mazurka also appears on galileo cd (GL 2) dated munich 1992

mazurka in a flat op 41 no 4

brescia	cd: foné 90F 32
23 june	cd: aura AUR 2082
1967	*foné dated 17 june 1967; aura is ussued as a*
	single cd and in an unnumbered set

mazurka in c op 56 no 2

munich	lp: dg 2530 236
october	lp: melodiya C10 19099-19100
1971	cd: dg 413 4492/447 6432
	cd: philips 456 9042

mazurka in f sharp minor op 59 no 3

brescia	cd: foné 90F 32
23 june	cd: aura AUR 2082
1967	*foné dated 17 june 1967; aura is issued as a*
	single cd and in an unnumbered set

chopin **mazurka in g minor op 67 no 2**

munich	lp: dg 2530 236
october	lp: melodiya C10 19099-19100
1971	cd: dg 413 4492/447 6432
	cd: philips 456 9042

bregenz	cd: aura AUR 2112/AUR 2272
20 march	*AUR 2112 is dated 3 march 1985 and is*
1985	*issued as single cd and in an unnumbered set*

a version of this mazurka also appears on galileo cd (GL 2) dated munich 1992

mazurka in a minor op 67 no 4

munich	lp: dg 2530 236
october	lp: melodiya C10 19099-19100
1971	cd: dg 413 4492/447 6432
	cd: philips 456 9042

mazurka in c op 68 no 1

munich	lp: dg 2530 236
october	lp: melodiya C10 19099-19100
1971	cd: dg 413 4492/447 6432
	cd: philips 456 9042

chopin **mazurka in a minor op 68 no 2**

milan 1941	78: hmv (italy) DA 5371 45: hmv (italy) ERQ 245/EQ 2123 lp: melodiya D 30749-30750 cd: piano library PL 252-255 cd: eremitage ERM 183 cd: magic talent CD 48050 cd: warner fonit 3984 269022 cd: hommage 700 1859/700 1850 cd: hall of fame 220017 *also issued by aura in an unnumbered set*
buenos aires 21 july 1949	cd: aura AUR 2172 *issued as single cd and in an unnumbered set*
turin december 1962	lp: rococo 2128 lp: discocorp IGI 350 lp: oversea 20115 lp: maison blanche MBL 1005.10 cd: cetra CDE 1042/CDAR 2002/AR 1 cd: eremitage ERM 122/ERM 301 cd: music and arts CD 924 cd: history 20.3169.360 cd: hommage 700 1859/700 1850 cd: aura AUR 2042 cd: warner fonit 0927 406472 *aura edition issued as single cd and in an* *unnumbered set; hommage and warner fonit* *editions are dated 1963*
brescia 23 june 1967	cd: aura AUR 2272
munich october 1971	lp: dg 2530 236 lp: melodiya C10 19099-19100 cd: dg 413 4492/447 6432 cd: philips 456 9042

chopin **mazurka in f minor op 68 no 4**

brescia	cd: foné 90F 32
23 june	cd: aura AUR 2082
1967	*foné edition dated 17 june 1967; aura edition*
	issued as single cd and in an unnumbered set

munich	lp: dg 2530 236
october	lp: melodiya C10 19099-19100
1971	cd: dg 413 4492/447 6432
	cd: philips 456 9042

prélude in c sharp minor op 45

munich	lp: dg 2530 236
october	lp: melodiya C10 19099-19100
1971	cd: dg 413 4492/447 6432
	cd: philips 456 9042

scherzo no 1 op 20

bregenz	cd: aura AUR 2062
15 january	*issued as single cd and in an unnumbered set*
1988	

london	cd: eremitage ERM 432
10 may	*also issued by aura in an unnumbered set*
1990	

chopin **scherzo no 2 op 31**

milan
1941

78: hmv (italy) DB 5355
45: hmv (italy) ERQ 296
lp: hmv (italy) QALP 10341
lp: emi 3C053 17017/3C153 50104-50106/
3C163 50104-50106/117 0171
lp: melodiya D 30749-30750
cd: eremitage ERM 183
cd: piano library PL 252-255
cd: magic talent CD 48050
cd: warner fonit 3984 269022
cd: hommage 700 1860/700 1850
cd: hall of fame 220017
also issued by aura in an unnumbered set

turin
december
1962

lp: discocorp IGI 350
lp: overesea 20114
cd: eremitage ERM 122/ERM 303
cd: cetra CDE 1021/CDAR 2002/AR 01
cd: music and arts CD 924
cd: history 20.3169.360
cd: hommage 700 1860/700 1850
cd: warner fonit 0927 406472
vhs video: rai VRN 2131
hommage and warner fonit editions are dated 1963

munich
october
1971

lp: dg 2530 236
lp: melodiya C10 19099-19100
cd: dg 413 4492/447 6432

bregenz
20 march
1985

cd: aura AUR 2112/AUR 2212
dated 3-7 march 1985; AUR 2112 is issued as
single cd and in an unnumbered set

chopin **valse in in a flat op 34 no 1**

turin

december

1962

lp: rococo 2128

lp: discocorp IGI 350

lp: paragaon LBI 53009/DSV 1001-1003

lp: discoreale 10072-10074

lp: oversea 20114

lp: maison blanche MBL 1005.10

cd: eremitage ERM 122/ERM 303

cd: cetra CDE 1042/CDAR 2002/
CDM 2040/AR 01

cd: music and arts CD 817/CD 924

cd: hommage 700 1859/700 1850

cd: aura AUR 2042

cd: warner fonit 0927 406472

vhs video: rai VRN 2130

hommage and warner fonit editions are dated 1963;
aura edition issued as single cd and in an unnumbered set

valse in a minor op 34 no 2

bregenz

15 january

1988

cd: aura AUR 2062

issued as single cd and in an unnumbered set

chopin **valse in in a flat op 69 no 1**

milan
1941

78: hmv (italy) DA 5371
lp: hmv (italy) QALP 10341
cd: eremitage ERM 183
cd: piano library PL 252-255
cd: magic talent CD 48050
cd: hommage 700 1859/700 1850
cd: hall of fame 220017
also issued by aura in an unnumbered set

turin
december
1962

lp: rococo 2128
lp: discocorp IGI 350
lp: paragon LBI 53009/DSV 1001-1003
lp: discoreale 10072-10073
lp: maison blanche MBL 1005.10
cd: cetra CDE 1042/CDAR 2002/
    CDM 2040/AR 01
cd: music and arts CD 817/CD 924
cd: history 20.3169.306
cd: eremitage ERM 122/ERM 302
cd: hommage 700 1859/700 1850
cd: aura AUR 2042
cd: warner fonit 0927 406472
vhs video: rai VRN 2130
hommage and warner fonit editions are dated 1963;
* aura edition is issued as a single cd and in an unnumbered set*

chopin **valse in e flat op posth (no 18)**

waesaw	lp: rococo 2122
13 march	lp: cetra LO 525
1955	lp: muza SX 1899
	cd: claque GM 1001
	cd: polskie nagrania PNCD 351
	cd: melodram MEL 28019

london	cd: testament SBT 2088
4 march	
1957	

turin	lp: rococo 2128
december	lp: discocorp IGI 350
1962	lp: paragon LBI 53009/DSV 1001-1003
	lp: discoreale 10072-10074
	lp: overesea 20114
	lp: maison blanche MBL 1005.10
	cd: eremitage ERM 122/ERM 302
	cd: cetra CDE 1042/CDAR 2002/
	CDM 2040/AR 01
	cd: music and arts CD 817/CD 924
	cd: hommage 700 1859/700 1850
	cd: aura AUR 2042
	cd: warner fonit 0927 406472
	hommage and warner fonit editions are dated 1963;
	aura edition issued as single cd and in an unnumbered set

MUZIO CLEMENTI (1752-1832)

piano sonata in b flat op 12 no 1

london
30 june
1959

lp: rococo 2088
lp: discocorp R 2088
lp: cls records RPCL 2008
lp: paragon LBI 53010/DSV 1001-1003
lp: discoreale 10072-10074
cd: music and arts CD 955/CD 4955

CLAUDE DEBUSSY (1862-1918)

children's corner (doctor gradus ad parnassum; jimbo's lullaby; serenade for a doll; the snow is dancing; the little shepherd; golliwog's cakewalk)

turin	lp: cetra LAR 33
august-	cd: cetra CDE 1048/CDAR 2005/AR 02
september	cd: history 20.3169.306
1962	cd: hommage 700 1851/700 1850
	cd: warner 0927 406492
	vhs video: rai VRN 2132
	some editions incorrectly dated 1963

lugano	cd: nuova era NE 2218
4 june	cd: memories HR 4368-4369
1968	

munich	lp: dg 2530 196
july	lp: melodiya C10 03747 000
1971	cd: dg 415 3722/447 6432/449 4382/
	459 0332/459 0692

hamburg	cd: memoria 999.101
7 may	*this set contains two versions of the same performance,*
1993	*described respectively as with and without technical*
	restoration; performance recorded at michelangeli's
	final public appearance

reflets dans l'eau/images livre 1

milan	78: hmv (italy) DB 6859
1941	45: hmv (italy) ERQ 247/7RQ 3017
	lp: hmv (italy) QALP 10341
	lp: emi 3C053 17017/3C153 50104-50106/
	3C163 50104-50106/117 0171
	lp: melodiya D 30749-30750
	cd: eremitage ERM 182
	cd: piano library PL 252-255
	cd: magic talent CD 48050
	cd: warner fonit 3984 269022
	cd: hommage 700 1851/700 1850
	cd: hall of fame 220017
	also issued by aura in an unnumbered set

debussy reflets dans l'eau/images livre 1 concluded
london   cd: testament SBT 2088
4 march 1957

turin   lp: cetra LAR 33
august-   lp: oversea 20112
september   lp: maison blanche MBL 1005.10
1962   cd: cetra CDE 1048/CDAR 2005
                                      cd: eremitage ERM 123/ERM 303
                                      cd: hommage 700 1851/700 1850
                                      cd: history 20.3169.306
                                      cd: warner 0927 406492
                                      vhs video: rai VRN 2132
                                      some editions incorrectly dated 1963

helsinki   lp: rococo 2073
22 may   cd: aura AUR 2182
1969   *aura edition is issued as a single cd and in a set*

munich   lp: dg 2530 196
july   lp: melodiya C10 03747 000
1971   cd: dg 415 3722/447 6432/449 4382/
                                        459 0332/459 0692
                                      cd: philips 456 9012

bern   cd: theatre (japan) 400 3535
18 march 1975

vatican city   cd: memoria ABM 999.001
13 june   cd: aura AUR 2022
1987   *aura edition is issued as a single cd and in a set*

hamburg   cd: memoria 999.101
7 may   *michelangeli's final public appearance*
1993

debussy **hommage a rameau/images livre 1**

warsaw	lp: rococo 2122
13 march	lp: cetra LO 525
1955	lp: muza SX 1898
	cd: polskie nagrania PNCD 351
	cd: melodram MEL 28019
london	cd: testament SBT 2088
4 march 1957	
turin	lp: cetra LAR 33
august-	lp: oversea 20112
september	lp: maison blanche MBL 1005.10
1962	cd: cetra CDE 1048/CDAR 2005
	cd: eremitage ERM 123/ERM 303
	cd: hommage 700 1851/700 1850
	cd: history 20.3169.306
	cd: warner 0927 406492
	vhs video: rai VRN 2132
	some editions incorrectly dated 1963
helsinki	lp: rococo 2073
22 may	cd: aura AUR 2182
1969	*aura edition is issued as a single cd and in an*
	unnumbered set
munich	lp: dg 2530 196
july	lp: melodiya C10 03747 000
1971	cd: dg 415 3722/447 6432/449 4382/
	459 0332/459 0692
	cd: philips 456 9012
bern	cd: theatre (japan) 400 3535
18 march 1975	
london	cd: bbc legends BBCL 40642
13 april 1982	
vatican city	cd: memoria ABM 999.001
13 june	cd: aura AUR 2022
1987	*aura edition is issued as a single cd and in an*
	unnumbered set
hamburg	cd: memoria 999.101
7 may 1993	*michelangeli's final public appearance*

debussy **mouvement/images livre 1**

turin	lp: cetra LAR 33
august	lp: oversea 20112
september	lp: maison blanche MBL 1005.10
1962	cd: cetra CDE 1048/CDAR 2005
	cd: eremitage ERM 123/ERM 303
	cd: hommage 700 1851/700 1850
	cd: history 20.3169.306
	cd: warner 0927 406492
	vhs video: rai VRN 2132
	some editions incorrectly dated 1963

helsinki	lp: rococo 2073
22 may	cd: aura AUR 2182
1969	*aura edition is issued as a single cd and in an unnumbered set*

munich	lp: dg 2530 196
july	lp: melodiya C10 03747 000
1971	cd: dg 415 3722/447 6432/ 449 4382/ 459 0332/459 0692
	cd: philips 456 9012

bern	cd: theatre (japan) 400 3535
18 march	
1975	

vatican city	cd: memoria ABM 999.001
13 june	cd: aura AUR 2022
1987	*aura edition is issued as a single cd and in an unnumbered set*

hamburg	cd: memoria 999.101
7 may	*michelangeli's final public appearance*
1993	

debussy **cloches a travers les feuilles/images livre 2**

london   cd: testament SBT 2088
3 march
1957

turin   lp: cetra LAR 33
august-   lp: oversea 20112
september   lp: maison blanche MBL 1005.10
1962   cd: cetra CDE 1048/CDAR 2005
                                         cd: eremitage ERM 123/ERM 303
                                         cd: hommage 700 1851/700 1850
                                         cd: history 20.3169.306
                                         cd: warner 0927 406492
                                         vhs video: rai VRN 2132
                                         some editions incorrectly dated 1963

helsinki   lp: rococo 2073
22 may   cd: aura AUR 2182
1969   *aura edition is issued as a single cd and in an*
                                         unnumbered set

munich   lp: dg 2530 196
july   lp: melodiya C10 03747 000
1971   cd: dg 415 3722/447 6432/ 449 4382/
                                             459 0332/459 0692
                                         cd: philips 456 9012

bern   cd: theatre (japan) 400 3535
18 march
1975

vatican city   cd: memoria ABM 999.001
13 june   cd: aura AUR 2022
1987   *aura edition is issued as a single cd and in an*
                                         unnumbered set

hamburg   cd: memoria 999.101
7 may   *michelangeli's final public appearance*
1993

debussy et la lune descend sur le temple qui fut/images livre 2

london	cd: testament SBT 2088
3 march	
1957	

turin	lp: cetra LAR 33
august-	lp: oversea 20112
september	lp: maison blanche MBL 1005.10
1962	cd: cetra CDE 1048/CDAR 2005
	cd: eremitage ERM 123/ERM 303
	cd: hommage 700 1851/700 1850
	cd: history 20.3169.306
	cd: warner 0927 406492
	vhs video: rai VRN 2132
	some editions incorrectly dated 1963

helsinki	lp: rococo 2073
22 may	cd: aura AUR 2182
1969	*aura edition is issued as a single cd and in an*
	unnumbered set

munich	lp: dg 2530 196
july	lp: melodiya C10 03747 000
1971	cd: dg 415 3722/447 6432/449 4382/
	459 0332/459 0692
	cd: philips 456 9012

bern	cd: theatre (japan) 400 3535
18 march	
1975	

vatican city	cd: memoria ABM 999.001
13 june	cd: aura AUR 2022
1987	*aura edition is issued as a single cd and in an*
	unnumbered set

hamburg	cd: memoria 999.101
7 may	*michelangeli's final public appearance*
1993	

debussy **poissons d'or/images livre 2**

turin	lp: cetra LAR 33
august-	lp: oversea 20112
september	lp: maison blanche MBL 1005.10
1962	cd: cetra CDE 1048/CDAR 2005
	cd: eremitage ERM 123/ERM 303
	cd: hommage 700 1851/700 1850
	cd: history 20.3169.306
	cd: warner 0927 406492
	vhs video: rai VRN 2132
	some editions incorrectly dated 1963
helsinki	lp: rococo 2073
22 may	cd: aura AUR 2182
1969	*aura edition is issued as a single cd and in an*
	unnumbered set
munich	lp: dg 2530 196
july	lp: melodiya C10 03747 000
1971	cd: dg 415 3722/447 6432/ 449 4382/
	459 0332/459 0692
	cd: philips 456 9012
bern	cd: theatre (japan) 400 3535
18 march	
1975	
vatican city	cd: memoria ABM 999.001
13 june	cd: aura AUR 2022
1987	*aura edition is issued as a single cd and in an*
	unnumbered set
hamburg	cd: memoria 999.101
7 may	*michelangeli's final public appearance*
1993	

both sets of images also published by brilliant classics 99228/99232 in a performance which they date as 1964

debussy **danseuses de delphes/préludes livre 1**

vatican city	cd: memoria ABM 999.001
29 april	cd: aura AUR 2012
1977	*aura edition issued as a single cd and in an* *unnumbered set*

hamburg	lp: dg 2531 200
june	cd: dg 413 4502/447 6432/449 4382
1978	cd: philips 456 9012

london	cd: bbc legends BBCL 40432
13 april	
1982	

hamburg	cd: memoria 999.101
7 may	*michelangeli's final public appearance*
1993	

voiles/préludes livre 1

vatican city	cd: memoria ABM 999.001
29 april	cd: aura AUR 2012
1977	*aura edition issued as a single cd and in an* *unnumbered set*

hamburg	lp: dg 2531 200
june	cd: dg 413 4502/447 6432/449 4382/
1978	459 0332/459 0692

london	cd: bbc legends BBCL 40432 ·
13 april	
1982	

hamburg	cd: memoria 999.101
7 may	*michelangeli's final public appearance*
1993	

debussy **le vent dans la pleine/préludes livre 1**

vatican city	cd: memoria ABM 999.001
29 april	cd: aura AUR 2012
1977	*aura edition issued as a single cd and in an unnumbered set*

hamburg	lp: dg 2531 200
june	cd: dg 413 4502/447 6432/449 4382
1978	

london	cd: bbc legends BBCL 40432
13 april	
1982	

hamburg	cd: memoria 999.101
7 may	*michelangeli's final public appearance*
1993	

les sons et les parfums tournent dans l'air du soir/préludes livre 1

vatican city	cd: memoria ABM 999.001
29 april	cd: aura AUR 2012
1977	*aura edition issued as a single cd and in an unnumbered set*

hamburg	lp: dg 2531 200
june	cd: dg 413 4502/447 6432/449 4382
1978	cd: philips 456 9012

london	cd: bbc legends BBCL 40432
13 april	
1982	

hamburg	cd: memoria 999.101
7 may	*michelangeli's final public appearance*
1993	

debussy **les collines d'anacapri/préludes livre 1**

vatican city	cd: memoria ABM 999.001
29 april	cd: aura AUR 2012
1977	*aurs edition issued as a single cd and in an unnumbered set*
hamburg	lp: dg 2531 200
june	cd: dg 413 4502/447 6432/449 4382/
1978	459 0332/459 0692
london	cd: bbc legends BBCL 40432
13 april	
1982	
hamburg	cd: memoria 999.101
7 may	*michelangeli's final public appearance*
1993	

des pas sur la neige/préludes livre 1

vatican city	cd: memoria ABM 999.001
29 april	cd: aura AUR 2012
1977	*aura edition issued as a single cd and in an unnumbered set*
hamburg	lp: dg 2531 200
june	cd: dg 413 4502/447 6432/449 4382/
1978	459 0332/459 0692
	cd: philips 456 9012
london	cd: bbc legends BBCL 40432
13 april	
1982	
hamburg	cd: memoria 999.101
7 may	*michelangeli's final public appearance*
1993	

debussy **ce qu'a vu le vent d'ouest/préludes livre 1**

vatican city	cd: memoria ABM 999.001
29 april	cd: aura AUR 2012
1977	*aurs edition issued as a single cd and in an*
	unnumbered set

hamburg	lp: dg 2531 200
june	cd: dg 413 4502/447 6432/449 4382/
1978	459 0332/459 0692

london	cd: bbc legends BBCL 40432
13 april	
1982	

hamburg	cd: memoria 999.101
7 may	*michelangeli's final public appearance*
1993	

la fille aux cheveux de lin/préludes livre 1

vatican city	cd: memoria ABM 999.001
29 april	cd: aura AUR 2012
1977	*aura edition issued as a single cd and in an*
	unnumbered set

hamburg	lp: dg 2531 200
june	cd: dg 413 4502/447 6432/449 4382/
1978	459 0332/459 0692
	cd: philips 456 9012

london	cd: bbc legends BBCL 40432
13 april	
1982	

hamburg	cd: memoria 999.101
7 may	*michelangeli's final public appearance*
1993	

debussy **la sérénade interrompue/préludes livre 1**

vatican city	cd: memoria ABM 999.001
29 april	cd: aura AUR 2012
1977	*aurs edition issued as a single cd and in an unnumbered set*

hamburg	lp: dg 2531 200
june	cd: dg 413 4502/447 6432/449 4382/
1978	459 0332/459 0692

london	cd: bbc legends BBCL 40432
13 april	
1982	

hamburg	cd: memoria 999.101
7 may	*michelangeli's final public appearance*
1993	

la cathédrale engloutie/préludes livre 1

vatican city	cd: memoria ABM 999.001
29 april	cd: aura AUR 2012
1977	*aura edition issued as a single cd and in an unnumbered set*

hamburg	lp: dg 2531 200
june	cd: dg 413 4502/447 6432/449 4382/
1978	459 0332/459 0692
	cd: philips 456 9012

london	cd: bbc legends BBCL 40432
13 april	
1982	

hamburg	cd: memoria 999.101
7 may	*michelangeli's final public appearance*
1993	

debussy **la danse de puck/préludes livre 1**

vatican city	cd: memoria ABM 999.001
29 april	cd: aura AUR 2012
1977	*aurs edition issued as a single cd and in an*
	unnumbered set

hamburg	lp: dg 2531 200
june	cd: dg 413 4502/447 6432/449 4382
1978	

london	cd: bbc legends BBCL 40432
13 april	
1982	

hamburg	cd: memoria 999.101
7 may	*michelangeli's final public appearance*
1993	

minstrels/préludes livre 1

vatican city	cd: memoria ABM 999.001
29 april	cd: aura AUR 2012
1977	*aura edition issued as a single cd and in an*
	unnumbered set

hamburg	lp: dg 2531 200
june	cd: dg 413 4502/447 6432/449 4382
1978	cd: philips 456 9012

london	cd: bbc legends BBCL 40432
13 april	
1982	

hamburg	cd: memoria 999.101
7 may	*michelangeli's final public appearance*
1993	

book 1 préludes planned by deutsche grammophon as both sound and video recording but filming was presumably not carried out debussy **brouillards/préludes livre 2**

stuttgart	cd: aura AUR 2102
27 october	*issued as single cd and in an unnumbered set*
1982	

bielefeld	cd: dg 427 3912/447 6432/449 4382
8 august	
1988	

feuilles mortes/préludes livre 2

stuttgart	cd: aura AUR 2102
27 october	*issued as single cd and in an unnumbered set*
1982	

bielefeld	cd: dg 427 3912/447 6432/449 4382
8 august	
1988	

la puerta del vino/préludes livre 2

stuttgart	cd: aura AUR 2102
27 october	*issued as single cd and in an unnumbered set*
1982	

bielefeld	cd: dg 427 3912/447 6432/449 4382
8 august	cd: philips 456 9012
1988	

les fées sont d'exquises danseuses/préludes livre 2

stuttgart	cd: aura AUR 2102
27 october	*issued as single cd and in an unnumbered set*
1982	

bielefeld	cd: dg 427 3912/447 6432/449 4382
8 august	
1988	

debussy **bruyeres/préludes livre 2**

turin	lp: cetra LAR 33
august-	cd: cetra CDE 1048/CDAR 2005/AR 02
september	cd: hommage 700 1851/700 1850
1962	cd: warner 0927 406492
	vhs video: rai VRN 2132
	some editions incorrectly dated 1963

stuttgart	cd: aura AUR 2102
27 october	*issued as single cd and in an unnumbered set*
1982	

bielefeld	cd: dg 427 3912/447 6432/449 4382
8 august	
1988	

général lavine eccentric/préludes livre 2

stuttgart	cd: aura AUR 2102
27 october	*issued as single cd and in an unnumbered set*
1982	

bielefeld	cd: dg 427 3912/447 6432/449 4382
8 august	cd: philips 456 9012
1988	

les terrasses des audiences au clair de lune/préludes livre 2

stuttgart	cd: aura AUR 2102
27 october	*issued as single cd and in an unnumbered set*
1982	

bielefeld	cd: dg 427 3912/447 6432/449 4382
8 august	cd: philips 456 9012
1988	

debussy **ondine/préludes livre 2**

stuttgart	cd: aura AUR 2102
27 october	*issued as single cd and in an unnumbered set*
1982	

bielefeld	cd: dg 427 3912/447 6432/449 4382
8 august	cd: philips 456 9012
1988	

homage a s. pickwick/préludes livre 2

stuttgart	cd: aura AUR 2102
27 october	*issued as single cd and in an unnumbered set*
1982	

bielefeld	cd: dg 427 3912/447 6432/449 4382
8 august	cd: philips 456 9012
1988	

canopes/préludes livre 2

turin	lp: cetra LAR 33
august-	cd: cetra CDE 1048/CDAR 2005/AR 02
september	cd: hommage 700 1851/700 1850
1962	cd: warner 0927 406492
	vhs video: rai VRN 2132
	some editions incorrectly dated 1963

stuttgart	cd: aura AUR 2102
27 october	*issued as single cd and in an unnumbered set*
1982	

bielefeld	cd: dg 427 3912/447 6432/449 4382
8 august	
1988	

les tierces alternées/préludes livre 2

stuttgart	cd: aura AUR 2102
27 october	*issued as single cd and in an unnumbered set*
1982	

bielefeld	cd: dg 427 3912/447 6432/449 4382
8 august	
1988	

debussy **feux d'artifice/préludes livre 2**

stuttgart	cd: aura AUR 2102
27 october	*issued as single cd and in an unnumbered set*
1982	
bielefeld	cd: dg 427 3912/447 6432/449 4382
8 august	cd: philips 456 9012
1988	

cassette tape of michelangeli playing debussy's épigraphes antiques in the version for solo piano may have been published in taiwan, although the work cannot be traced in listings of the pianist's repertory

CESAR FRANCK (1822-1890)

variations symphoniques pour piano et orchestre

los angeles	los angeles	lp: cls records RPCL 2028
13-16	philharmonic	lp: discocorp OPUS 73
january	wallenstein	cd: as-disc AS 321
1949		cd: notes PGP 11027
		cd: aura AUR 2152
		aurs edition is issued as single cd and in an
		unnumbered set

BALDASSARE GALUPPI (1706-1785)

piano sonata in c

turin	cd: nuova era NE 2218
december	cd: cetra CDE 1042
1962	cd: arkadia CDGI 904
	vhs video: rai VRN 2129
	arkadia edition is described as rome 13 august 1963

rome	lp: decca LXT 6181/SXL 6181/414 0651
4march	lp: london (usa) CM 9446/CS 6446
1965	lp: telefunken SMD 1199/641.302/
	641.551AN
	cd: decca 417 7722
	cd: philips 456 9012
	private recording arranged by michelangeli

presto/piano sonata in g minor

milan	78: hmv (italy) DB 6859
1941	45: hmv (italy) 7RQ 3017
	lp: hmv (italy) QALP 10341
	lp: emi 3C053 17017/3C153 50104-50106/
	3C163 50104-50106/117 0171
	lp: melodiya D 26603-26604
	cd: eremitage ERM 183
	cd: piano library PL 252-255
	cd: magic talent CD 48050
	cd: warner fonit 3984 269022
	cd: hommage 700 1860/700 1850
	cd: hall of fame 220017
	also issued by aura in an unnumbered set

buenos aires	cd: aura AUR 2172
21 july	*issued as a single cd and in an unnumbered set*
1949	

ENRIQUE GRANADOS (1867-1916)

andaluza/danzas espanolas
milan
1939

78: hmv (italy) DB 5354
78: victor 12-0730
45: hmv (italy) EQ 3170/ERQ 270
lp: hmv (italy) QALP 10341
lp: emi 3C053 17017/3C153 50104-50106/
    3C163 50104-50106/117 0171
lp: melodiya D 30749-30750
cd: emi CDH 764 4902
cd: piano library PL 252-255
cd: eremitage ERM 183
cd: arkadia CD 624/CDHP 624/78563
cd: hommage 700 1859/700 1850
cd: hall of fame 220017
also issued by aura in an unnumbered set

EDVARD GRIEG (1843-1907)

piano concerto

geneva	suisse romande	cd: eremitage ERM 183
7 june	orchestra	cd: piano library PL 252-253
1941	ansermet	cd: magic talent CD 48071
		cd: warner fonit 3894 269012
		cd: hommage 700 1853/700 1850
		also issued by aura in an unnumbered set; all editions comprise only a 3'27" fragment from the first movement (bulk of the recording presumably lost)

milan	la scala	78: telefunken SKB 3280-3283
9 february	orchestra	lp: telefunken 641.903 AJ
1942	galliera	lp: rococo 2125
		lp: cls records RPCL 2006
		cd: piano library PL 183/PL 252-253
		cd: classico PTC 2005
		cd: teldec 843.765/0630 133032/9031 764392
		cd: magic talent CD 48058
		cd: hommage 700 1853/700 1850
		cd: cantus classics CACD 50011
		cd: aura AUR 2152
		cd: hall of fame 220017
		aura edition issued as single cd and in unnumbered set

rome	rai roma	lp: cetra LAR 44
27 june	orchestra	cd: arkadia CD 507/CDHP 507
1963	rossi	cd: frequenz 041.009
		cd: nuova era NE 013.6341
		cd: memories HR 4368-4369
		cd: green line CD3CLC 4005
		cd: notablu 935.1103-1104

london	new	lp: rococo 2061
17 june	philharmonia	lp: discocorp DIS 3701
1965	frühbeck	cd: bbc legends BBCL 40432
	de burgos	

stuttgart	sdr orchestra	cd: arlecchino ARLA 06
28 november	celibidache	*incorrectly dated 28 october 1973*
1973		

deutsche grammophon planned a recording of the concerto in 1984 in conjunction with concert performances with orchestre de paris conducted by barenboim, but this did not materialise

grieg **erotic/lyric pieces op 43**

milan

6 september

1942

78: telefunken SKB 3283

lp: rococo 2125

cd: piano library PL 211/PL 252-253

cd: teldec 4509 936712/0630 133032

cd: magic talent CD 48071

cd: classico PTC 2005

cd: simax PSC 1809

cd: pearl GEMMCDS 9086

cd: arkadia CD 624/CDHP 624

cd: hommage 700 1858/700 1850

cd: hall of fame 220017

melancholy/lyric pieces op 47

milan

1939

78: hmv (italy) DA 5379

cd: piano library PL 252-255

cd: emi CDH 764 4902

cd: eremitage ERM 183

cd: arkadia 78563

cd: warner fonit 3984 269012

cd: simax PSC 1809

cd: notablu 935.1103-1104

cd: hommage 700 1858/700 1850

cd: hall of fame 220017

also issued by aura in an unnumbered set

buenos aires

21 july

1949

cd: aura AUR 2172

issued as single cd and in an unnumbered set

grieg **cradle song/lyric pieces op 68**

milan	78: hmv (italy) DA 5379
1939	cd: piano library PL 252-255
	cd: emi CDH 764 4902
	cd: eremitage ERM 183
	cd: arkadia CD 624/CDHP 624/78563
	cd: warner fonit 3894 269012
	cd: simax PSC 1809
	cd: notablu 935.1103-1104
	cd: hommage 700 1858/700 1850
	cd: hall of fame 220017
	also issued by aura in an unnumbered set

buenos aires	cd: aura AUR 2172
21 july	*issued as single cd and in an unnumbered set*
1949	

stuttgart	cd: arlecchino ARLA 06
28 november	*incorrectly dated 28 october 1973*
1973	

FRANZ JOSEF HAYDN (1732-1809)

piano concerto no 4 in g

lugano	zürich chamber	lp: rococo 2076
5 april	orchestra	
1974	de stoutz	

thun	zürich chamber	lp: emi ASD 3128/1C065 02614/
january	orchestra	2C069 02614/3C065 02614/
1975	de stoutz	EG 29 08551
		lp: angel 37136
		lp: melodiya C10 17873 000
		cd: emi CDC 749 3242

piano concerto no 11 in d

turin	rai torino	lp: cetra LAR 44/AR 02
18 december	orchestra	lp: cls records RPCL 2008
1959	rossi	cd: cetra CDAR 2006
		cd: movimento musica 051.050
		cd: hommage 700 1852/700 1850
		cd: warner fonit 0927 406482

brescia	orchestra	lp: everest olympic 8142
22 june	"gasparo da	lp: discocorp SID 712
1964	salo"	lp: curcio CON 23
	orizio	cd: music and arts CD 296/CD 4296
		cd: arkadia CD 560/CDHP 560
		incorrectly described by discocorp and music and arts
		as piano concerto no 2 in d; all editions given various
		incorrect dates in 1967 and 1968

thun	zürich chamber	lp: emi ASD 3124/1C065 02614/
january	orchestra	2C069 02614/3C065 02614/
1975	de stoutz	EG 29 08551
		lp: angel 37136
		lp: melodiya C10 17873 000
		cd: emi CDC 749 3242

FRANZ LISZT (1811-1886)

piano concerto no 1

geneva	suisse romande	cd: piano library PL 252-255
7 august	orchestra	cd: eremitage ERM 183
1939	ansermet	cd: arkadia CD 624/CDHP 624
		cd: magic talent CD 48050
		cd: warner fonit 3894 269012
		cd: hommage 700 1853/700 1850
		cd: hall of fame 220017
		dated by piano library and hommage as 8 july 1939;
		all issues have first 36 bars of first movement missing

florence	maggio	lp: cetra DOC 64/DOC 1001
17 june	musicale	
1953	orchestra	
	mitropoulos	

turin	rai torino	lp: cetra LAR 12
28 april	orchestra	lp: cls records RPCL 2028
1961	kubelik	lp: laudis CM 1004
		lp: joker SM 1333
		lp: discocorp RR 495
		lp: movimento musica 01.004
		cd: movimento musica 051.050
		cd: cetra CDAR 2004/AR 01
		cd: frequenz 041.009
		cd: bramante BLICD 7004
		cd: arkadia CD 507/CDHP 507
		cd: hommage 700 1854/700 1850
		cd: warner fonit 0927 406502

tokyo	yomiuri	lp: discocorp OPUS 73
9 april	symphony	cd: aura AUR 2082
1965	rohan	*aura edition issued as single cd and in an unnumbered*
		set but incorrectly dated 4 april 1965

liszt **totentanz for piano and orchestra**

turin	rai torino	lp: cetra TRV 1001
28 april	orchestra	lp: laudis CM 1004
1961	kubelik	lp: joker SM 1333
		lp: cls records RPCL 2028
		lp: discocorp RR 495
		lp: movimento musica 01.004
		cd: bramante BLICD 7004
		cd: arkadia CD 507/CDHP 507
vatican city	rai roma	cd: memoria ABM 999.001
28 may	orchestra	
1962	gavazzeni	

eglogue/années de pelerinage suisse

stuttgart	cd: aura AUR 2102
27 october	*issued as single cd and in an unnumbered set*
1982	

FRANCOIS MARESCOTTI (1902-1998)

fantasque
milan
1941

78: hmv (italy) DB 5354/DB 6859
78: victor 12-0730
lp: hmv (italy) QALP 10341
lp: emi 3C053 17017/3C153 50104-50106/
    3C163 50104-50106/117 0171
lp: melodiya D 30749-30750
cd: piano library PL 252-255
cd: eremitage ERM 183
cd: magic talent CD 48050
cd: warner fomit 3984 269022
cd: hommage 700 1860/700 1850
cd: hall of fame 220017

FEDERICO MOMPOU (1893-1987)

cancion y danza no 1
milan
1942

78: hmv (italy) DA 5432
cd: emi CDH 764 4902
cd: piano library PL 252-255
cd: warner fonit 3984 269022
cd: hommage 700 1859/700 1850
cd: philips 456 9042
cd: hall of fame 220017

warsaw
13 march
1955

lp: rococo 2122
lp: cetra LO 525
lp: muza SX 1899
cd: claque GM 1001
cd: polskie nagrania PNCD 351
cd: melodram MEL 28019

cancion/cancion y danza no 6
london
4 march
1957

cd: testament SBT 2088

WOLFGANG AMADEUS MOZART (1756-1791)

piano concerto no 13 k415

rome 15 december 1951	rai roma orchestra giulini	lp: cetra LAR 26 lp: music masters MJA 1969.2 cd: movimento musica 051.050 cd: cetra CDE 1002/CDAR 2001/AR 01 cd: hommage 700 1856/700 1850
naples 29 november 1953	alessandro scarlatti orchestra caracciolo	lp: emi 27 01911 cd: emi CDH 763 8192
naples 23 july 1958	rai napoli orchestra caracciolo	lp: everest olympic 8142 lp: discocorp SID 712 lp: replica RPL 2457-2459 lp: melodiya M10 44853 000 lp: movimento musica 01.020 cd: movimento musica 011.011 cd: greenline CD3CLC 4005 cd: curcio CON 27
brescia 25 may 1968	orchestra "gaspare da salo" orizio	cd: arkadia CD 560/CDHP 560 cd: sarpe CD 7005
hamburg january 1990	ndr orchestra garben	lp: dg 431 0971 cd: dg 431 0972/447 6432

mozart **piano concerto no 15 k450**

milan	orchestra	78: hmv DB 11348-11350
26 27	pomeriggi	lp: hmv (italy) QALP 5345/QALP 10408
june	musicali	lp: emi 3C053 00656/3C153 50104-50106/
1951	gracis	3C163 50104-50106/100 6561
		cd: emi CDH 763 8192/CDH 769 2412/
		CDE 575 2302
		cd: piano library PL 252-255
		piano library incorrectly dated 1947

turin	rai torino	lp: discocorp RR 422
23 december	orchestra	lp: cls records RPCL 2001
1955	rossi	lp: replica RPL 2457-2459
		lp: movimento musica 01.020
		cd: movimento musica 051.050/011.011/ANF 34.1
		cd: cetra CDE 1021/CDAR 2004
		cd: notablu 935.1091-1092
		cd: hommage 700 1856/700 1850

lugano	italian-swiss	lp: concordia CMS 1001
21 june	radio	cd: andromeda ANR 2503/NAS 2601
1956	orchestra	cd: theatre (japan) 400.3535
	scherchen	

lugano	zürich chamber	lp: rococo 2076
5 april	orchestra	cd: aura AUR 2202
1974	de stoutz	*aura edition issued as single cd and in an unnumbered set*

hamburg	ndr orchestra	lp: dg 431 0971
february	garben	cd: dg 431 0972/447 6432
1990		

mozart **piano concerto no 20 k466**

rome 15 december 1951	rai roma orchestra giulini	lp: cetra LAR 26 cd: cetra CDE 1002/CDAR 2001/AR 02 cd: movimento musica 051.050 cd: curcio CON 01 cd: notablu 935.1091-1092 cd: hommage 700 1857/700 1850 cd: urania awaiting publication
florence 17 june 1953	maggio musicale orchestra mitropoulos	lp: cetra DOC 64/DOC 1001 cd: arkadia CD 552/CDHP 552 cd: discantus (greece) 189.6162
turin 18 december 1959	rai torino orchestra rossi	lp: discocorp RR 422 lp: cls records RPCL 2001 lp: movimento musica 01.070 cd: movimento musica 011.009 cd: cetra CDE 1021
vatican city 11 october 1966	orchestra "gasparo da salo" orizio	cd: arkadia CD 560/CDHP 560
bremen 9 june 1989	ndr orchestra garben	lp: dg 429 3531 cd: dg 429 3532/447 6432

rehearsal extracts on 2 pianos (garben plays second piano) on sampler cd accompanying cord garben's book "arturo benedetti michelangeli: gratwanderungen mit einem genie" (europäische verlagsanstalt 2002)

cd with this concerto may have appeared on the esquire label (595.9966) with rai napoli orchestra conducted by caracciolo and dated 23 july 1958, but the concerto played at a concert on that date was no 15 k450

mozart **piano concerto no 23 k488**

rome	rai roma	lp: cetra LAR 26/TRV 1001
15 december	orchestra	lp: cls records RPCL 2002
1951	giulini	lp: music masters MJA 1969.2
		lp: movimento musica 01.070
		cd: movimento musica 051.050/011.009
		cd: cetra CDAR 2004/AR 02
		cd: hommage 700 1857/700 1850
		cd: urania awaiting publication

naples	orchestra	lp: emi 27 01911/29 10891
23-28	alessandro	cd: emi CDH 763 8192
november	scarlatti	
1953	caracciolo	

piano concerto no 25 k503

bremen	ndr orchestra	lp: dg 429 3531
9 june	garben	cd: dg 429 3532/447 6432
1989		

piano quartet in e flat k493

croisiere	wallez, violin	cd: aura AUR 2202
paquet	joubert, viola	*recorded during a mediterranean cruise;*
renaissance	dariel, cello	*issued as single cd and in an unnumbered set*
9 september		
1972		

SERGEI RACHMANINOV (1873-1943)

piano concerto no 4

london	philharmonia	lp: hmv ALP 1538/ASD 255
7-10	gracis	lp: hmv (italy) QALP 10196/ASDQ 5257
march		lp: hmv (france) FALP 533/ASDF 142/
1957		CVD 1533
		lp: electrola E 90914/STE 90914
		lp: angel 34459/35567
		lp: melodiya D 9359-9360
		lp: emi 1C053 00140/3C053 00140/
		3C153 50104-50106/3C163 50104-50106/
		SXLP 30169/100 1401
		cd: emi CDC 749 3262/CDM 567 2382

MAURICE RAVEL (1875-1937)

piano concerto in g

london	philharmonia	lp: hmv ALP 1538/ASD 255
7-10	gracis	lp: hmv (italy) QALP 10196/ASDQ 5257
march		lp: hmv (france) FALP 533/ASDF 142/
1957		CVD 1533
		lp: electrola E 90914/STE 90914
		lp: angel 34459/35567
		lp: melodiya D 9305-9306
		lp: emi 1C053 00140/3C053 00140/
		3C153 50104-50106/3C163 50104-50106/
		SXLP 30169/100 1401
		cd: emi CDC 749 3262/CDM 567 2382
		cd: philips 456 9012
milan	rai milano	lp: cls records RPCL 2007
march	orchestra	
1957	gracis	
turin	rai torino	lp: cetra LAR 44/LAR 47
12 december	orchestra	lp: discocorp RR 495
1961	sanzogno	lp: replica RPL 2457-2459
		cd: arkadia CD 904/CDGI 904
		replica and arkadia issues are dated january 1952
london	london	cd: arlecchino ARLA 79
8 april	symphony	cd: exclusive EX 92T 61-62
1982	celibidache	*also unpublished video recording*
munich	munich	cd: galileo GL 02
5 june	philharmonic	
1992	celibidache	

ravel **gaspard de la nuit**

london	lp: cls records RPCL 2004
30 june	lp: discoreale 10072-10074
1959	lp: paragon DSV 1001-1003
	lp: discocorp R 2088
	lp: grandi concerti GCL 22
	cd: music and arts CD 955/CD 4955
	cd: philips 456 9012
	cd: bbc legends BBCL 40642

prague	cd: music and arts CD 817
20 may	cd: multisonic 31.01932
1960	*also issued by toshiba in japan*

lugano	lp: discocorp RR 404
4 june	cd: nuova era NE 2218
1968	cd: memories HR 4368-4369

helsinki	lp: rococo 2073
22 may	cd: arkadia CD 904/CDGI 904
1969	

vatican city	cd: memoria ABM 999.001
13 june	cd: aura AUR 2042
1987	*aura edition issued as single cd and in an unnumbered set*

valses nobles et sentimentales

arezzo	lp: cetra LO 517/DOC 46
12 february	lp: cls records RPCL 2007
1952	cd: arkadia CD 904/CDGI 904

tokyo	lp: rococo 2112
29 october	
1973	

DOMENICO SCARLATTI (1685-1757)

sonata in d-dminor k 9/L 413

milan	78: hmv (italy) DA 5380
1942	45: hmv (italy) ERQ 270
	lp: hmv (italy) QALP 10431
	lp: rococo 2125
	lp: emi 3C053 17017/3C153 50104-50106/
	3C163 50104-50106/117 0171
	lp: melodiya D 26603-26604
	cd: emi CDH 764 4902
	cd: arkadia CD 624/CDHP 624/78563
	cd: piano library PL 252-255
	cd: warner fonit 3984 269022
	cd: hommage 700 1858/700 1850
	cd: hall of fame 220017
warsaw	lp: cetra LO 525
13 march	lp: paragon LBI 53010/DSV 1001-1003
1955	lp: discoreale 10072-10074
	lp: muza SX 1899
	cd: polskie nagrania PNCD 351
	cd: melodram MEL 28019
helsinki	cd: aura AUR 2182
22 may	*issued as single cd and in an unnumbered set*
1969	

scarlatti **sonata in c minor k 11/L 352**

milan 1942	78: hmv (italy) DA 5380
	45: hmv (italy) ERQ 270
	lp: hmv (italy) QALP 10341
	lp: rococo 2125
	lp: emi 3C053 17017/3C153 50104-50106/ 3C163 50104-50106/117 0171
	cd: emi CDH 764 4902
	cd: arkadia CD 624/CDHP 624/78563
	cd: piano library PL 252-255
	cd: warner fonit 3984 269022
	cd: hommage 700 1858/700 1850
	cd: hall of fame 220017
warsaw 27 february 1955	lp: cetra LO 525
	lp: rococo 2122
	lp: paragon LBI 53010/DSV 1001-1003
	lp: discoreale 10072-10074
	lp: muza SX 1899
	cd: polskie nagrania PNCD 351
	cd: melodram MEL 28019
turin december 1962	cd: cetra CDE 1048
	cd: nuova era NE 2218
	vhs video: rai VRN 2129
rome 4march 1965	lp: decca LXT 6181/SXL 6181/414 0651
	lp: london (usa) CM 9446/CS 6446
	lp: telefunken SMD 1199/641.302/641 551AN
	cd: decca 417 7722
	cd: philips 456 9012
	private recording arranged by michelangeli
helsinki 22 may 1969	cd: aura AUR 2182
	issued as single cd and in an unnumbered set
bregenz 15 january 1988	cd: aura AUR 2062
	issued as single cd and in an unnumbered set

scarlatti **sonata in b minor k 27/L 449**

milan	78: telefunken SKB 3290
20 january	lp: rococo 2125
1943	cd: piano library PL 183/PL 252-255
	cd: pearl GEMMCDS 9086
	cd: classico PTC 2005
	cd: magic talent CD 48071
	cd: teldec 0630 133032/4509 936712
	cd: hommage 700 1858/700 1850
	cd: philips 464 3812
	cd: hall of fame 220017
1949	vhs video: warner/nvc 3984 291993
	dvd video: warner/nvc 3984 291992
arezzo	lp: cetra LO 517/DOC 46
12 february	
1952	
warsaw	lp: cetra LO 525
13 march	lp: paragon LBI 53010/DSV 1001-1003
1955	lp: discoreale 10072 10074
	lp: rococo 2122
	lp: muza SX 1899
	cd: claque GM 1001
	cd: polskie nagrania PNCD 351
	cd: melodram MEL 28019
turin	cd: cetra CDE 1048
december	cd: nuova era NE 2218
1962	vhs video: rai VRN 2129
helsinki	cd: aura AUR 2182
22 may	*issued as single cd and in an unnumbered set*
1969	
bregenz	cd: aura AUR 2062
15 january	*issued as single cd and in an unnumbered set*
1988	

scarlatti **sonata in e k29/L 461**
arezzo
12 february
1952

lp: cetra LO 517/DOC 46
cd: aura AUR 2262

sonata in d k96/L 465
milan
20 january
1943

78: telefunken SKB 3290
lp: rococo 2125
cd: piano library PL 183/PL 252-253
cd: pearl GEMMCDS 9086
cd: classico PTC 2005
cd: arkadia CD 624/CDHP 624/78563
cd: teldec 0630 133032/4509 936712
cd: magic talent CD 48071
cd: hommage 700 1858/700 1850
cd: hall of fame 220017

sonata in c k159/L 104
turin
december
1962

cd: cetra CDE 1048
cd: nuova era NE 2218
vhs video: rai VRN 2129

rome
4march
1965

lp: decca LXT 6181/SXL 6181/414 0651
lp: london (usa) CM 9446/CS 6446
lp: telefunken SMD 1199/641.302/
    641.551AN
cd: decca 417 7722
cd: philips 456 9012
private recording arranged by michelangeli

helsinki
22 may
1969

cd: aura AUR 2182
issued as single cd and in an unnumbered set

scarlatti **sonata in d k322/L 483**

arezzo
12 february
1952

lp: cetra LO 517/DOC 46
cd: aura AUR 2262

warsaw
13 march
1955

lp: cetra LO 525
lp: paragon LBI 53010/DSV 1001-1003
lp: discoreale 10072-10074
lp: muza SX 1899
cd: polskie nagrania PNCD 351
cd: melodram MEL 28019

turin
december
1962

cd: cetra CDE 1048
cd: nuova era NE 2218
vhs video: rai VRN 2129

rome
4 march
1965

lp: decca LXT 6181/SXL 6181/414 0651
lp: london (usa) CM 9446/CS 6446
lp: telefunken SMD 1191/641.302/
      641.551AN
lp: melodiya D 26603-26604
cd: decca 417 7722
cd: philips 456 9012
private recording arranged by michelangeli

helsinki
22 may
1969

cd: aura AUR 2182
issued as single cd and in an unnumbered set

bregenz
15 january
1988

cd: aura AUR 2062
issued as single cd and in an unnumbered set

FRANZ SCHUBERT (1797-1828)

piano sonata in a minor d537

bern	lp: rococo 2117
18 march	lp: discocorp IGI 334
1975	

hamburg	lp: dg 2532 017
february	cd: dg 400 0432/447 6432/457 7622
1981	

lugano	cd: aura AUR 2192
7 april	*issued as single cd and in an unnumbered set*
1981	

ROBERT SCHUMANN (1810-1856)

piano concerto

milan	la scala	78: telefunken SKB 3260-3263
9 april	orchestra	lp: telefunken 641.903AJ
1942	pedrotti	cd: teldec 843.765/0630 133032/ 9031 764392
		cd: piano library PL 211/PL 252-255
		cd: magic talent CD 48058
		cd: cantus classics CACD 50012
		cd: hommage 700 1854/700 1850
		cd: hall of fame 220017
		cantus classics incorrectly name conductor as galliera

new york	new york	lp: rococo 2024/2057
21 november	philharmonic	lp: arioso 15006
1948	mitropoulos	cd: as-disc AS 321
		cd: historic performers HP 21
		cd: piano library PL 272
		cd: notes PGP 11027
		cd: aura AUR 2152
		aura edition issued as single cd and in an *unnumbered set*

warsaw	warsaw	lp: rococo 2122
27 march	philharmonic	lp: cetra LO 525
1955	rowicki	lp: joker SM 1329
		lp: muza SX 1897
		cd: polskie nagrania PNCD 328 ·
		cd: melodram MEL 28019

turin	rai torino	lp: rococo 2061
23 december	orchestra	lp: discocorp DIS 3701
1955	rossi	lp: cls records RPCL 2006
		lp: movimento musica 01.018
		lp: replica RPL 2457-2459
		cd: frequenz 041.009
		frequenz issue names conductor as gracis and is dated *14 march 1955*

schumann piano concerto/concluded

lugano	swiss-italian	lp: concordia CMS 1001
21 june	radio	cd: andromeda ANR 2503/NAS 2601
1956	orchestra	cd: theatre (japan) 400.3535
	scherchen	
vatican city	rai roma	lp: cetra LAR 44
28 april	orchestra	cd: cetra CDAR 2003/AR 01
1962	gavazzeni	cd: arkadia CD 505/CDHP 505
		cd: movimento musica 051.050
		cd: nuova era 013.6341
		cd: memoria ABM 999.001
		cd: history 20.3169.306
		cd: hommage 700 1852/700 1850
		cd: warner fonit 0927 406502
stockholm	swedish radio	cd: arkadia CD 592/CDHP 592/LE 951
19 november	orchestra	
1967	celibidache	
paris	orchestre	dg unpublished
3-4	de paris	*grieg concerto also planned for these concerts*
october	barenboim	*but did not take place*
1984		
munich	munich	cd: concert artists' recordings FED 027
25 september	philharmonic	
1992	celibidache	

schumann **three pieces from album für die jugend: matrosenlied; winterzeit I; winterzeit II**

thun	lp: emi ASD 3129/1C065 02613/2C069 02613/
january	3C065 02613
1975	lp: angel 32149/37137
	lp: melodiya C10 17897 000
	cd: emi CDC 749 3252
	cd: philips 456 9042

carnaval

london	lp: bbc records REGL 431
4 march	lp: dg 2531 090/2536 415
1957	lp: replica RPL 2468
	lp: movimento musica 01.018
	lp: discocorp RR 402
	cd: greenline CD3CLC 4005
	cd: dg 423 2312/447 6432
	cd: philips 456 9042
	cd: testament SBT 2088

prague	cd: multisonic 31.01932
30 may	*also issued by toshiba in japan*
1957	

thun	lp: emi ASD 3129/1C065 02613/2C069 02613/
january	3C065 02613
1975	lp: angel 32149/37137
	lp: melodiya C10 17897 000
	cd: emi CDC 749 3252

schumann **faschingsschwank aus wien**

warsaw 13 march 1955	lp: rococo 2122 lp: cetra LO 525 lp: paragon DSV 1001-1003 lp: discoreale 10072-10074 lp: joker SM 1329 lp: grandi concerto GCL 11 cd: classico PTC 2018 cd: polskie nagrania PNCD 351 cd: melodram MEL 28019
london 4 march 1957	lp: bbc records REGL 431 lp: dg 2531 090/2536 415 lp: discocorp RR 402 lp: replica RPL 2468 cd: dg 423 2312/447 6432 cd: greenline CD3CLC 4005 cd: notablu 935.1103-1104 cd: testament SBT 2088
helsinki 22 may 1969	cd: aura AUR 2182 *issued as single cd and in an unnumbered set*
tokyo 29 october 1973	lp: rococo 2112

performance of the work on 4 june 1968 is issued on aura AUR 2222 but no concert can be traced as having taken place on that date

PELLEGRINO TOMEONI (1729-1816)

allegro

milan
22 january
1943

78: telefunken SKB 3321
lp: rococo 2125
cd: pearl GEMMCDS 9086
cd: classico PTC 2005
cd: piano library PL 211/PL 252-255
cd: magic talent CD 48071
cd: teldec 0630 133032/4509 936712
cd: hommage 700 1860/700 1850
cd: hall of fame 220017

ANTONIO VIVALDI (1678-1741)

allegro from concerto in b minor, arranged by tamburini

geneva
11 november
1942

suisse romande
orchestra
ansermet

cd: eremitage ERM 183
cd: piano library PL 252-255
cd: magic talent CD 48050
cd: warner fonit 3984 269022
cd: hommage 700 1854/700 1850
cd: hall of fame 220017

alfred cortot

1877-1962

ISAAC ALBENIZ (1860-1909)

malaguena/recuerdos de viaje

new york 11 january 1919	78: victor 560/64846 78: hmv DA 144 cd: music and arts CD 615 cd: biddulph LHW 014-015 cd: pearl GEMMCD 9386
camden nj 22 april 1920	78: victor 560/64846 *re-recording to replace 11 january 1919 version*
camden nj 28 february 1923	cd: biddulph LHW 014-015 *unpublished victor 78rpm recording*
paris 2 june 1930	78: hmv DA 1121 78: victor 1581 cd: biddulph LHW 020 cd: dante HPC 089-090 cd: music and arts CD 615

seguidilla/cantos de espana

camden nj
7 january
1919

78: victor 560/64819
78: hmv DA 144
  cd: music and arts CD 615
cd: biddulph LHW 014-015

camden nj
22 april
1920

78: victor 560/64819
re-recording to replace 7 january 1919 version

camden nj
28 february
1923

cd: biddulph LHW 014-015
unpublished victor 78rpm recording

london
5 december
1924

hmv unpublished

paris
2 june
1930

78: hmv DA 1121
78: victor 1581
cd: biddulph LHW 020
cd: dante HPC 089-090
cd: music and arts CD 615

bajo la palmera/cantos de espana

1920

duo-art piano roll
lp: decca SDDR 173

london
5 december
1924

hmv unpublished

camden nj
27 october
1926

78: victor 1271
cd: biddulph LHW 020

triana/iberia

camden nj
1922

cd: biddulph LHW 014-015
unpublished victor 78rpm recording

JOHANN SEBASTIAN BACH (1685-1750)

toccata and fugue in d minor, arranged by cortot
london   hmv unpublished
20 april
1948

arioso from harpsichord concerto in f minor, arranged by cortot
london   78: hmv DB 3262
18 may   78: victor 14612
1937   lp: toshiba GR 2211
                                cd: biddulph LHW 020
                                cd: emi CHS 567 2112

london   78: hmv DA 1898
19 april   lp: hmv ALP 1197
1948

organ concerto in d minor after vivaldi, arranged by cortot
london   78: hmv DB 3261-3262
18 may   78: victor M 573
1937   lp: toshiba GR 2211
                                cd: biddulph LHW 020
                                cd: emi CHS 567 2112

brandenburg concerto no 1
paris   école   78: hmv DB 2033-2034
1 june   normale   78: victor 11781-11782
1933   orchestra   lp: toshiba GR 2211
                 cortot conducts   cd: emi CHS 567 2112

brandenburg concerto no 2
paris   école   78: hmv DB 2035-2036
30 may-   normale   78: victor 11930-11931
2 june   orchestra   lp: toshiba GR 2211
1933   *cortot conducts*   cd: emi CHS 567 2112

bach **brandenburg concerto no 3**

paris	école	78: hmv DB 1259-1260
2 december	normale	78: victor 4225-4226
1931	orchestra	lp: toshiba GR 2211
	cortot conducts	cd: emi CHS 567 2112

brandenburg concerto no 4

paris	école	78: hmv DB 2037-2038
29 may	normale	78: victor 7915-7916
1933	orchestra	lp: toshiba GR 2211
	bouillon, violin	cd: emi CHS 567 2112
	cortet and	
	morseau, flutes	
	cortot conducts	

brandenburg concerto no 5

paris	école	78: hmv DB 1783-1784
16-18	normale	78: victor 7863-7864
may	orchestra	lp: toshiba GR 2211
1932	thibaud, violin	cd: emi CHS 567 2112
	cortet, flute	
	cortot conducts and	
	is piano soloist	

brandenburg concerto no 6

paris	école	78: hmv DB 1626-1627
2 december	normale	78: victor 11264-11265
1931	orchestra	lp: toshiba GR 2211
	cortot conducts	cd: emi CHS 567 2112

LUDWIG VAN BEETHOVEN (1770-1827)

piano sonata no 1
paris   hmv unpublished
6 january
1958

paris   hmv unpublished
1 junc
1959

paris   hmv unpublished
11-12
january
1960

paris   hmv unpublished
15 january
1960

paris   hmv unpublished
3 june
1960

beethoven **piano sonata no 2**

paris   hmv unpublished
8 january
1958

paris   hmv unpublished
1 june
1959

paris   hmv unpublished
12 january
1960

paris   hmv unpublished
15 january
1960

paris   hmv unpublished
3 june
1960

beethoven **piano sonata no 3**
paris   hmv unpublished
8 january
1958

paris   hmv unpublished
1 june
1959

paris   hmv unpublished
12 january
1960

paris   hmv unpublished
15 january
1960

paris   hmv unpublished
3 june
1960

piano sonata no 4
paris   hmv unpublished
9 january
1958

paris   hmv unpublished
1 june
1959

paris   hmv unpublished
15 january
1960

paris   hmv unpublished
13 june
1960

beethoven **piano sonata no 5**

paris   hmv unpublished
9 january
1958

paris   hmv unpublished
2 june
1959

paris   hmv unpublished
13 january
1960

paris   hmv unpublished
18 january   *recording incomplete*
1960

paris   hmv unpublished
13 june
1960

beethoven piano sonata no 6
paris   hmv unpublished
9 january
1958

paris   hmv unpublished
2 june
1959

paris   hmv unpublished
13 january
1960

paris   hmv unpublished
18 january   *recording incomplete*
1960

paris   hmv unpublished
13 june
1960

piano sonata no 7
paris   hmv unpublished
9 january
1958

paris   hmv unpublished
2 june
1959

paris   hmv unpublished
13 january
1960

paris   hmv unpublished
18 january   *recording incomplete*
1960

paris   hmv unpublished
14 june
1960

beethoven **piano sonata no 8 "pathétique"**

paris	hmv unpublished
11 january	
1958	

paris	hmv unpublished
3 june	
1959	

paris	hmv unpublished
13 january	
1960	

paris	hmv unpublished
18 january	
1960	

paris	hmv unpublished
14 june	
1960	

beethoven **piano sonata no 9**

paris	hmv unpublished
11 january	
1958	

paris	hmv unpublished
3 june	
1959	

paris	hmv unpublished
13 january	
1960	

paris	hmv unpublished
18 january	*recording incomplete*
1960	

paris	hmv unpublished
14 june	*recording incomplete*
1960	

piano sonata no 10

paris	hmv unpublished
11 january	
1958	

paris	hmv unpublished
3 june	
1959	

paris	hmv unpublished
13 january	
1960	

paris	hmv unpublished
18 january	*recording incomplete*
1960	

paris	hmv unpublished
14 june	*recording incomplete*
1960	

beethoven **piano sonata no 11**

paris   hmv unpublished
11 january
1958

paris   hmv unpublished
4 june
1959

piano sonata no 12 "funeral march"

paris   hmv unpublished
11 january
1958

paris   hmv unpublished
4 june
1959

piano sonata no 13

paris   hmv unpublished
13 january
1958

paris   hmv unpublished
4 june
1959

piano sonata no 14 "moonlight"

paris   hmv unpublished
13 january
1958

paris   hmv unpublished
4 june
1959

beethoven piano sonata no 15
paris   hmv unpublished
13 january
1958

paris   hmv unpublished
5 june
1959

piano sonata no 16
paris   hmv unpublished
13 january
1958

paris   hmv unpublished
5 june
1959

piano sonata no 17 "tempest"
paris   hmv unpublished
12 14
march
1958

paris   hmv unpublished
5 june
1959

piano sonata no 18
paris   hmv unpublished
21 march
1958

paris   hmv unpublished
5 june
1959

beethoven **piano sonata no 19**

paris	hmv unpublished
21 march	
1958	

paris	hmv unpublished
8 june	
1959	

piano sonata no 20

paris	hmv unpublished
21 march	
1958	

paris	hmv unpublished
8 june	
1959	

piano sonata no 21 "waldstein"

paris	hmv unpublished
21 march	
1958	

paris	hmv unpublished
8 june	
1959	

piano sonata no 22

paris	hmv unpublished
21 march	
1958	

paris	hmv unpublished
8 june	
1959	

beethoven **piano sonata no 23 "appassionata"**

paris	hmv unpublished
21 march	
1958	

paris	hmv unpublished
8 june	
1959	

piano sonata no 24

paris	hmv unpublished
24 march	
1958	

paris	hmv unpublished
9 june	
1959	

piano sonata no 25

paris	hmv unpublished
24 march	
1958	

paris	hmv unpublished
9 june	
1959	

piano sonata no 26

paris	hmv unpublished
24 march	
1958	

paris	hmv unpublished
9 june	
1959	

piano sonata no 27

paris	hmv unpublished
24 march	
1958	

paris	hmv unpublished
9 june	
1959	

beethoven **piano sonata no 28**

paris 10-16 june 1959	hmv unpublished

piano sonata no 30

march 1927	duo-art piano roll 7109-7110 cd: nimbus NI 8814
paris 10-16 june 1959	hmv unpublished

piano sonata no 31

paris 15-16 june 1959	hmv unpublished

piano sonata no 32

paris 15-16 june 1959	hmv unpublished

violin sonata no 5 "kreutzer"

paris 27-28 may 1929	thibaud, violin	78: hmv DB 1328-1331 78: victor M 86 lp: hmv COLH 92 lp: angel GR 50012 cd: emi CDH 764 0572 cd: biddulph LAB 028

beethoven **piano trio no 5**

london	thibaud, violin	hmv unpublished
6 july	casals, cello	*recording incomplete: only one 78rpm side*
1926		*recorded*

piano trio no 7 "archduke"

london	thibaud, violin	78: hmv DB 1223-1227
14-18	casals, cello	78: victor M 92
november		lp: hmv COLH 29
1928		lp: emi 1C047 00857M/2C051 00857/
		2C061 00857M/3C161 50089-50091M
		lp: world records SH 230
		cd: emi CDH 761 0242/CDM 566 9862/
		CHS 764 0572
		cd: monopoly GI 20059
		second movement
		cd: emi CMS 566 1822

variations for cello and piano on mozart's bei männern welche liebe fühlen

london	casals, cello	78: hmv DA 915-916
21 june		78: victor 3047-3048
1927		lp: hmv COLH 92
		lp: emi 1C147 01538-01539M/HLM 7106/
		RLS 723/1C153 52475-52477M
		cd: emi CHS 764 0572
		cd: pearl GEMMCDS 9461/GEMMCDS 9935

adagio, variations and rondo for violin, cello and piano on ich bin der schneider kakadu

london	thibaud, violin	lp: emi RLS 723/1C153 52475-52477M
5-6	casals, cello	lp: world records SH 230
july		cd: emi CHS 764 0572
1926		cd: naxos 811.0188
		unpublished hmv 78rpm recording

JOHANNES BRAHMS (1833-1897)

double concerto

barcelona	pau casals	78: hmv DB 1311-1314
10-11	orchestra	78: victor M 99
may	thibaud, violin	lp: hmv COLH 75
1929	casals, cello	lp: emi 1C053 03034M/HLM 7104/
	cortot conducts	RLS 723/1C153 52475-52477M
		lp: toshiba GR 2011
		cd: emi CHS 764 0572
		cd: pearl GEMMCD 9363/
		GEMMCDS 9935
		cd: koch 3-7705-2
		cd: dutton CDEA 5006
		cd: naxos 811.0930

wiegenlied, arranged by cortot

new york	78: victor 1271
21 march	78: hmv DA 691
1925	cd: biddulph LHW 020
	cd: piano library PL 214
	cd: pearl GEMMCD 9386

london	78: hmv DA 1923
20 april	lp: hmv ALP 1197
1948	

tokyo	78: victor (japan) SF 727
1-3	cd: venezia (japan) V 1003
december	
1952	

EMMANUEL CHABRIER (1841-1894)

idylle no 6/scenes pittoresques

september	piano roll 6910
1925	cd: nimbus NI 8814

ERNEST CHAUSSON (1855-1899)

concerto for violin, piano and string quartet

paris	thibaud, isnard	78: hmv DB 1649-1653
1 july	and voulfman,	78: victor 8240-8244
1931	violins	lp: emi 2C051 03719
	blanpain, viola	lp: toshiba GR 2133
	eisenberg, cello	cd: biddulph LAB 029

FREDERIC CHOPIN (1810-1849)

piano concerto no 2

london	orchestra	78: hmv DB 2612-2615/
8 july	barbirolli	DB 8658-8661 auto
1935		78: victor M 567
		lp: emi 3C153 53540-53546M
		lp: angel GR 70021
		cd: emi CZS 767 3592
		cd: pearl GEMMCD 9491
		cd: grammofono AB 78501/AB 78516
		cd: music and arts CD 718
		cd: naxos 811.0612

piano sonata no 2 "funeral march"

london   hmv unpublished
5 december
1927

london   78: hmv DB 1250-1251
4-5   lp: discocorp RR 227
june   cd: biddulph LHW 001
1928   *recording completed on 11 december 1928*

london   78: hmv DB 2019-2020
8 july   lp: hmv (france) FALP 376
1933   lp: emi 3C153 53540-53546M/
                                   1C047 01400M
                              cd: emi CZS 767 3592
                              cd: brilliant classics 99228/99230
                              cd: music and arts CD 717
                              cd: grammofono AB 78516

paris   hmv unpublished
5 march
1943

tokyo   78: victor (japan) SD 3098-3099
1-3   lp: victor (japan) RA 2087
december   cd: toshiba shinseido SGR 8113
1952

london   hmv unpublished
7-8
may
1953

munich   lp: replica RPL 2479
8 april
1956

paris   hmv unpublished
28 december
1956

chopin **piano sonata no 3**

paris	hmv unpublished
21 may	*recording incomplete*
1930	

london	78: hmv DA 1209-1212
12 may	lp: discocorp RR 227
1931	cd: biddulph LHW 001
	cd: emi CZS 767 3592
	cd: music and arts CD 717

london	78: hmv DA 1333-1336
6 july	78: victor M 142
1933	lp: emi 3C153 53540-53546M/
	1C047 01504M
	lp: angel 60241

paris	hmv unpublished
7 december	*recording completed on 25 february 1943*
1942	

paris	hmv unpublished
27 december	
1956	

paris	hmv unpublished
5 february	
1957	

chopin **andante spianato et grande polonaise**

november	duo-art piano roll 6365
1920	lp: decca SDDR 173
	cd: nimbus NI 8814

camden nj	78: victor 6358/78421
5 february	cd: pearl GEMMCD 9386
1923	cd: piano library PL 214
	cd: biddulph LHW 014-015
	polonaise section only recorded

tokyo	78: victor (japan) SD 3100
1-3	cd: venezia (japan) V 1003
december	
1952	

chopin **ballade no 1 op 23**

camden nj	cd: biddulph LHW 020
21 march	cd: pearl GEMMCD 9386/GEMMCD 9491
1925	cd: music and arts CD 4622
	unpublished victor 78rpm recording

new york	78: victor 6612
27 december	78: hmv DB 853
1926	cd: emi CZS 767 3592
	cd: biddulph LHW 020
	cd: piano library PL 214
	cd: music and arts CD 317
	cd: pearl GEMMCD 9386

london	78: hmv DB 1343
7 june	78: victor M 94
1929	lp: discocorp RR 317
	cd: biddulph LHW 001
	cd: music and arts CD 317/CD 4871

london	78: hmv DB 2023
6-7	78: victor M 198
july	lp: hmv COLH 91
1933	lp: emi 3C153 53540-53546M
	lp: angel GR 70024
	cd: emi CZS 767 3592

paris	hmv unpublished
5 march	*recording completed on 22 september 1943*
1943	

london	hmv unpublished
28 june	
1954	

paris	hmv unpublished
28 december	
1956	

chopin **ballade no 2 op 38**

london 11 march 1929	78: hmv DB 1344 78: victor M 94 lp: discocorp RR 317 cd: biddulph LHW 001 cd: music and arts CD 317/CD 1871
london 6-7 july 1933	78: hmv DB 2024 78: victor M 198 lp: hmv COLH 91 lp: emi 3C153 53540-53546M lp: angel GR 70024 cd: emi CZS 767 3592
paris 5 march 1943	hmv unpublished *recording completed on 22 september 1943*
paris 28 december 1956	hmv unpublished

chopin **ballade no 3 op 47**

london	78: hmv DB 1345
11 march	78: victor M 94
1929	lp: discocorp RR 317
	cd: biddulph LHW 001
	cd: music and arts CD 317/CD 1871

london	78: hmv DB 2025
6-7	78: victor M 198
july	lp: hmv COLH 91
1933	lp: emi 3C153 53540-53546M
	lp: angel GR 70024
	cd: emi CZS 767 3592/CHS 764 0572

paris
5 march
1943

hmv unpublished
recording completed on 22 september 1943

paris
28 december
1956

hmv unpublished

chopin **ballade no 4 op 52**

london	78: hmv DB 1346
11 march	78: victor M 94
1929	lp: discocorp RR 317
	cd: biddulph LHW 001
	cd: music and arts CD 317/CD 1871

london	78: hmv DB 2026
6-7	78: victor M 198
july	lp: hmv COLH 91
1933	lp: emi 3C153 53540-53546M
	lp: angel GR 70024
	cd: emi CZS 767 3592

paris	hmv unpublished
5 march	*recording completed on 22 september 1943*
1943	

paris	hmv unpublished
28 december	
1956	

chopin **barcarolle in f sharp**

london 5 july 1933	78: hmv DB 2030 lp: emi 3C153 53540-53546M lp: angel GR 70022 cd: emi CZS 767 3592/CDH 761 0502 cd: music and arts CD 717
london 17 october 1951	45: victor WHMV 1032 lp: victor LHMV 1032 lp: hmv (france) FALP 376 lp: emi 1C047 01400
paris 28 december 1956	hmv unpublished

chopin berceuse in d flat

camden nj	78: victor 6063/74623
27 january	78: hmv DB 167
1920	cd: emi CZS 767 3592
	cd: piano library PL 214
	cd: pearl GEMMCD 9386
	cd: biddulph LHW 014-015

new york	78: victor 6752
28 december	78: hmv DB 1145
1926	lp: discocorp RR 227
	cd: emi CZS 767 3592
	cd: biddulph LHW 020
	cd: music and arts CD 317/CD 4871

london	hmv unpublished
5 july	
1933	

paris	hmv unpublished
10 september	
1943	

london	78: hmv DB 21175
4 november	45: victor WCT 60
1949	45: hmv (germany) 7RF 238
	lp: victor LCT 1038
	lp: hmv ALP 1197
	lp: hmv (france) FALP 349
	lp: hmv (italy) QALP 10080
	lp: emi 3C153 53540-53546M
	lp: angel GR 70024

chopin **spring, arranged by liszt/19 polish songs**

london	78: hmv DA 1682
10 march	lp: emi HQM 1182/3C153 53540-53546M
1939	lp: world records SH 327
	cd: emi CZS 767 3592
	cd: pearl GEMMCD 9491
	cd: music and arts CD 462

my joys, arranged by liszt/19 polish songs

camden nj	78: victor 562/64973
28 january	78: hmv DA 146
1919	cd: piano library PL 214
	cd: pearl GEMMCD 9386
	cd: biddulph LHW 014-015

camden nj	78: victor 562/64973
28 february	cd: emi CZS 767 3592
1923	cd: biddulph LHW 014-015
	cd: music and arts CD 615
	re recording to replace 28 january 1919 version

london	cd: biddulph LHW 020
10 march	*unpublished hmv 78rpm recording*
1939	

the ring, arranged by liszt/19 polish songs

london	78: hmv DA 1682
10 march	lp: emi HQM 1182/3C153 53540-53546M
1939	lp: world records SH 327
	cd: emi CZS 767 3592
	cd: pearl GEMMCD 9491
	cd: music and arts CD 462

3 écossaises op 72

paris	hmv unpublished
10 september	
1943	

london	hmv unpublished
20 april	
1948	

chopin étude op 10 no 1

london
4-15
july
1933

78: hmv DB 2027
78: victor M 398
lp: hmv COLH 39
lp: hmv (france) FJLP 5050
lp: emi 3C153 53540-53546M
lp: angel GR 70025
cd: emi CZS 767 3592
cd: philips 456 7512

paris
2 november
1942

78: hmv (france) W 1531
cd: emi CZS 767 3592

london
29 june
1954

hmv unpublished

this étude was also played by cortot for a 1928 silent film, which is published by warner/nvc on vhs video 3984 291993 and on dvd video 3984 291992

étude op 10 no 2

london
4-15
july
1933

78: hmv DB 2027
78: victor M 398
lp: hmv COLH 39
lp: hmv (france) FJLP 5050
lp: emi 3C153 53540-53546M
lp: angel GR 70025
cd: emi CZS 767 3592
cd: philips 456 7512

paris
2 november
1942

78: hmv (france) W 1532
cd: emi CZS 767 3592

london
29 june
1954

hmv unpublished

chopin **étude op 10 no 3**

london	78: hmv DB 2028
4-15	78: victor M 398
july	lp: hmv COLH 39
1933	lp: hmv (france) FJLP 5050
	lp: emi 3C153 53540-53546M
	lp: angel GR 70025
	cd: emi CZS 767 3592
	cd: philips 456 7512

paris	78: hmv (france) W 1531
2 november	cd: emi CZS 767 3592
1942	

london	78: hmv DB 21521
16 october	45: victor WHMV 1032
1951	lp: victor LHMV 1032

tokyo	78: victor (japan) SD 3101
1-3	lp: victor (japan) LS 103/RA 2087
december	cd: toshiba shinseido SGR 8113
1952	

london	hmv unpublished
29 june	
1954	

chopin **étude op 10 no 4**
london
4-15
july
1933

78: hmv DB 2027
78: victor M 398
lp: hmv COLH 39
lp: hmv (france) FJLP 5050
lp: cmi 3C153 53540-53546M
lp: angel GR 70025
cd: cmi CZS 767 3592
cd: philips 456 7512

paris
2 november
1942

78: hmv (france) W 1531
cd: emi CZS 767 3592

london
16 october
1951

78: hmv DB 21521
45: victor WHMV 1032
lp: victor LHMV 1032

london
29 june
1954

hmv unpublished

chopin **étude op 10 no 5**

camden nj	78: victor 64989
22 april	78: hmv DA 145
1920	cd: biddulph LHW 014-015
january	duo-art piano roll
1923	cd: nimbus NI 8814
camden nj	78: victor 64989
28 february	cd: emi CZS 767 3592
1923	cd: biddulph LHW 014-015
	re-recording to replace 22 april 1920 version
london	78: hmv DB 2027
4-15	78: victor M 398
july	lp: hmv COLH 39
1933	lp: hmv (france) FJLP 5050
	lp: emi 3C153 53540-53546M
	lp: angel GR 70025
	cd: emi CZS 767 3592
	cd: philips 456 7512
paris	78: hmv (france) W 1532
2 november	cd: emi CZS 767 3592
1942	
london	lp: hmv ALP 1197
29 june	lp: hmv (france) FALP 349
1954	

chopin **étude op 10 no 6**
london
4-15
july
1933

78: hmv DB 2028
78: victor M 398
lp: hmv COLH 39
lp: hmv (france) FJLP 5050
lp: cmi 3C153 53549-53546M
lp: angel GR 70025
cd: cmi CZS 767 3592
cd: philips 456 7512

paris
2 november 1942

78: hmv (france) W 1533
cd: emi CZS 767 3592

london
29 june 1954
étude op 10 no 7
london
4-15
july
1933

hmv unpublished

78: hmv DB 2027
78: victor M 398
lp: hmv COLH 39
lp: hmv (france) FJLP 5050
lp: emi 3C153 53540-53546M
lp: angel GR 70025
cd: emi CZS 767 3592
cd: philips 456 7512

paris
2 november 1942

78: hmv (france) W 1532
cd: cmi CZS 767 3592

london
29 june 1954
étude op 10 no 8
london
4-15
july
1933

hmv unpublished

78: hmv DB 2029
78: victor M 398
lp: hmv COLH 39
lp: hmv (france) FJLP 5050
lp: emi 3C153 53540-53546M
lp: angel GR 70025
cd: emi CZS 767 3592
cd: philips 456 7512

paris
2 november 1942

78: hmv (france) W 1532
cd: cmi CZS 767 3592

london
29 june 1954

hmv unpublished

chopin **étude op 10 no 9**

london
4-15
july
1933

78: hmv DB 2029
78: victor M 398
lp: hmv COLH 39
lp: hmv (france) FJLP 5050
lp: emi 3C153 53540-53546M
lp: angel GR 70025
cd: emi CZS 767 3592
cd: philips 456 7512

paris
2 november 1942

78: hmv (france) W 1532
cd: emi CZS 767 3592

london
29 junc 1954

hmv unpublished

étude op 10 no 10

london
4-15
july
1933

78: hmv DB 2029
78: victor M 398
lp: hmv COLH 39
lp: hmv (france) FJLP 5050
lp: emi 3C153 53540-53546M
lp: angel GR 70025
cd: emi CZS 767 7512
cd: philips 456 7512

paris
2 novembcr 1942

78: hmv (france) W 1533
cd: emi CZS 767 3592

london
29 junc 1954

hmv unpublished

étude op 10 no 11

london
4-15
july
1933

78: hmv DB 2028
78: victor M 398
lp: hmv COLH 39
lp: hmv (france) FJLP 5050
lp: emi 3C153 53540-53546M
lp: angel GR 70025
cd: emi CZS 767 7512
cd: philips 456 7512

paris
2 novembcr 1942

78: hmv (france) W 1533
cd: emi CZS 767 3592

london
29 junc 1954

hmv unpublished

chopin **étude op 10 no 12**

london	78: hmv DB 2029
4-15	78: victor M 398
july	lp: hmv COLH 39
1933	lp: hmv (france) BJLP 5050
	lp: emi 3C153 53540-53546M
	lp: angel GR 70025
	cd: emi CZS 767 3592
	cd: philips 456 7512

paris	78: hmv (france) W 1533
2 november 1942	cd: emi CZS 767 3592

london	hmv unpublished
29 june 1954	

complete set of op 10 études recorded on 4-15 july 1933 also issued on lp by world records SH 326

étude op 25 no 1

new york	78: victor 1101
21 march	78: hmv DA 691
1925	cd: biddulph LHW 020
	cd: music and arts CD 4871
	cd: emi CZS 767 3592
	cd: piano library PL 214
	cd: pearl GEMMCD 9386
	cd: biddulph LHW 014-015

london	78: hmv DB 2308
18-21	lp: hmv COLH 39
june	lp: hmv (france) FJLP 5050
1934	lp: emi 3C153 53540-53546M
	lp: angel GR 70025
	cd: emi CZS 767 3592
	cd: philips 456 7512

paris	78: hmv (france) W 1534
4 november 1942	cd: emi CZS 767 3592

london	hmv unpublished
29 june 1954	

chopin **étude op 25 no 2**

london	78: hmv DB 2308
18-21	lp: hmv COLH 39
june	lp: hmv (france) FJLP 5050
1934	lp: emi 3C153 53540-53546M
	lp: angel GR 70025
	cd: emi CZS 767 3592
	cd: biddulph LHW 014-015
	cd: philips 456 7512

paris	78: hmv (france) W 1534
4 november 1942	cd: emi CZS 767 3592

london	78: hmv DB 21521
16 october	45: victor WHMV 1032/EHA 14
1951	lp: victor LHMV 1032
	lp: hmv ALP 1197
	lp: hmv (france) FALP 349
	lp: hmv (italy) QALP 10080

london	hmv unpublished
29 june 1954	

étude op 25 no 3

london	78: hmv DB 2309
10 june	lp: hmv COLH 39
1934	lp: hmv (france) FJLP 5050
	lp: emi 3C153 53540-53546M
	lp: angel GR 70025
	cd: emi CZS 767 3592
	cd: philips 456 7512

paris	78: hmv (france) W 1535
4 november 1942	cd: emi CZS 767 3592

london	hmv unpublished
29 june 1954	

étude op 25 no 4
london
10 june
1934

78: hmv DB 2309
lp: hmv COLH 39
lp: hmv (france) FJLP 5050
lp: emi 3C153 53540-53546M
lp: angel GR 70025
cd: emi CZS 767 3592
cd: philips 456 7512

paris
4 november 1942

78: hmv (france) W 1535
cd: emi CZS 767 3592

london
29 june 1954

hmv unpublished

étude op 25 no 5
london
18-21
june
1934

78: hmv DB 2309
lp: hmv COLH 39
lp: hmv (france) FJLP 5050
lp: emi 3C153 53540-53546M
lp: angel GR 70025
cd: emi CZS 767 3593
cd: philips 456 7512

paris
4 november 1942

78: hmv (france) W 1535
cd: emi CZS 767 3592

london
29 june 1954

hmv unpublished

étude op 25 no 6
london
18-21
june
1934

78: hmv DB 2309
lp: hmv COLH 39
lp: hmv (france) FJLP 5050
lp: emi 3C153 53540 53546M
lp: angel GR 70025
cd: emi CZS 767 3592
cd: philips 456 7512

paris
4 november 1942

78: hmv (france) W 1535
cd: emi CZS 767 3592

london
29 june 1954

hmv unpublished

chopin **étude op 25 no 7**

london	78: hmv DB 2310
18-21	lp: hmv COLH 39
june	lp: hmv (france) FJLP 5050
1934	lp: emi 3C153 53540-53546M
	lp: angel GR 70025
	cd: emi CZS 767 3592
	cd: philips 456 7512

paris	78: hmv (france) W 1535
4 november	cd: emi CZS 767 3592
1942	

london	hmv unpublished
29 june	
1954	

étude op 25 no 8

april	duo-art piano roll 6740
1924	cd: nimbus NI 8814

london	78: hmv DB 2309
10 june	lp: hmv COLH 39
1934	lp: hmv (france) FJLP 5050
	lp: emi 3C153 53540-53546M
	lp: angel GR 70025
	cd: emi CZS 767 3592
	cd: philips 456 5712

paris	78: hmv (france) W 1535
4 november	cd: emi CZS 767 3592
1942	

london	hmv unpublished
29 june	
1954	

chopin **étude op 25 no 9**

camden nj	78: victor 64989
22 april	78: hmv DA 145
1920	cd: biddulph LHW 014-015

january	duo-art piano roll 6593
1923	cd: nimbus NI 8814
	cd: biddulph LWH 014-015

camden nj	78: victor 64989
28 february	cd: emi CZS 767 3592
1923	cd: biddulph LWH 014-015
	re-recording to replace 22 april 1920 version

london	78: hmv DB 2310
18-21	lp: hmv COLH 39
june	lp: hmv (france) FJLP 5050
1934	lp: emi 3C153 53540-53546M
	lp: angel GR 70025
	cd: emi CZS 767 3592
	cd: philips 456 7512

paris	78: hmv (france) W 1534
4 november	cd: emi CZS 767 3592
1942	

tokyo	78: victor (japan) SF 727
1-3	lp: victor (japan) LS 103/RA 2087
december	
1952	

london	lp: hmv ALP 1197
29 june	lp: hmv (france) FALP 349
1954	lp: hmv (italy) QALP 10080

chopin **étude op 25 no 10**

london	78: hmv DB 2308
18-21	lp: hmv COLH 39
june	lp: hmv (france) FJLP 5050
1934	lp: emi 3C153 53540-53546M
	lp: angel GR 70025
	cd: emi CZS 767 3592
	cd: philips 456 7512

| paris | 78: hmv (france) W 1534 |
| 4 november 1942 | cd: emi CZS 767 3592 |

| london | hmv unpublished |
| 29 june 1954 | |

étude op 25 no 11

camden nj	78: victor 6417/74829
1 march	cd: emi CZS 767 3592
1923	cd: pearl GEMMCD 9386
	cd: piano library PL 214
	cd: biddulph LHW 014-015

march	duo-art piano roll
1923	lp: decca SDDR 173
	cd: nimbus NI 8814

london	78: hmv DB 2310
18-21	lp: hmv COLH 39
june	lp: hmv (france) FJLP 5050
1934	lp: emi 3C153 53540-53546M
	lp: angel GR 70025
	cd: emi CZS 767 3592
	cd: philips 456 7512

| paris | 78: hmv (france) W 1534 |
| 2 november 1942 | cd: emi CZS 767 3592 |

| london | hmv unpublished |
| 29 june 1954 | |

chopin **étude op 25 no 12**

january 1927	duo-art piano roll 7088 cd: nimbus NI 8814
london 18-21 june 1934	78: hmv DB 2308 lp: hmv COLH 39 lp: hmv (france) FJLP 5050 lp: emi 3C153 53540-53546M lp: angel GR 70025 cd: emi CZS 767 3592 cd: philips 456 7512
paris 4 november 1942	78: hmv (france) W 1534 cd: emi CZS 767 3592
london 29 june 1954	hmv unpublished

complete set of op 25 études recorded in june 1934 also issued on lp by world records SH 327

trois nouvelles études

london 10 october 1947	cd: music and arts CD 615 cd: appian APR 5571 *unpublished hmv 78rpm recording*
london 4 november 1949	78: hmv DB 21070 lp: hmv (france) FALP 376 lp: emi 3C153 53540-53546M/ 1C047 01400M cd: emi CZS 767 3592

chopin **fantasy in f minor**

london	78: hmv DB 2031-2032
4 july	78: victor 8250-8251
1933	lp: hmv COLH 91
	lp: emi 3C153 53540-53546M
	lp: angel GR 70025
	cd: emi CZS 767 3592
	cd: music and arts CD 717
	cd: grammofono AB 78516

paris	hmv unpublished
7 july	
1943	

tokyo	78: victor (japan) SD 3109
1-3	lp: victor (japan) JAS 273/LS 2029
december	cd: toshiba shinseido SGR 8114
1952	

paris	hmv unpublished
28 december	
1956	

fantasy impromptu in c sharp minor

london	78: hmv DB 2022
5 july	78: victor 8329
1933	lp: hmv COLH 38
	lp: emi 3C153 53540-53546M
	lp: angel GR 70027
	cd: emi CDH 761 0502

paris	hmv unpublished
10 september	
1943	

impromptu no 1

camden nj
28 december
1922

78: victor 6417/74830
cd: emi CZS 767 3592
cd: pearl GEMMCD 9386
cd: piano library PL 214
cd: biddulph LHW 014-015

london
5 july
1933

78: hmv DB 2021
78: victor 8238
lp: hmv COLH 38
lp: emi 3C153 53540-53546M/
    1C047 00889M
lp: angel GR 70027
cd: emi CDH 761 0502

paris
10 september
1943

hmv unpublished

chopin **impromptu no 2**

new york	78: victor 6502
21 march	78: hmv DB 853
1925	cd: pearl GEMMCD 9386
	cd: piano library PL 214
	cd: music and arts CD 4871
	cd: biddulph LHW 020
	cd: emi CZS 767 3592
	cd: biddulph LHW 014-015
	first electrical recording by victor to be issued in usa

london	78: hmv DB 2021
5 july	78: victor 8238
1933	lp: hmv COLH 38
	lp: emi 3C153 53540-53546M/
	1C047 00889M
	lp: angel GR 70027
	cd: emi CDH 761 0502

paris	hmv unpublished
10 september	
1943	

tokyo	78: victor (japan) SD 3102
1-3	lp: victor (japan) LS 2001/RA 2087
december	cd: toshiba shinseido SGR 8113
1952	

impromptu no 3

may	duo-art piano roll 7327
1929	cd: nimbus NI 8814

london	78: hmv DB 2022
5 july	78: victor 8239
1933	lp: hmv COLH 38
	lp: emi 3C153 53540-53546M/
	1C047 00889M/HLM 7008
	lp: angel GR 70027
	cd: emi CZS 767 3592/CHS 761 0502

paris	hmv unpublished
10 september	
1943	

chopin **mazurkas, complete set**

paris   hmv unpublished
15 october
1957

nocturnc op 9 no 2
london   78: hmv DB 1321
13 march   lp: cmi 3C153 53540-53546M/
1929   HLM 7008
                               lp: angel GR 70027
                               lp: discocorp RR 227
                               cd: emi CZS 767 3592
                               cd: biddulph LHW 001
                               biddulph issue is dated 19 march 1929

london   78: hmv DB 21018
4 november   45: hmv (france) 7RF 239
1949   45: victor WHMV 1032
                               lp: hmv (france) FALP 376
                               lp: victor LHMV 1032
                               lp: emi 1C047 01400M

tokyo   78: victor (japan) SD 3102
1-3   lp: victor (japan) LS 103/RA 2087
december   cd: toshiba shinseido SGR 8113
1952

paris   hmv unpublished
6-11
june
1957

chopin **nocturne op 15 no 1**

london   hmv unpublished
4 november
1949

london   78: hmv DB 21417
17 october   45: hmv 7R 162
1951   45: hmv (france) 7RF 265
          45: hmv (italy) 7RQ 265
          45: electrola 7RW 147
          45: victor WHMV 1032/EHA 14
          lp: hmv (france) FALP 376
          lp: victor LHMV 1032
          lp: emi 3C153 53540-53546M/
            1C047 01400M
          cd: emi CZS 767 3592

paris   hmv unpublished
6-11
june
1957

nocturne op 15 no 2

london   78: hmv DA 1923
19 april   lp: hmv ALP 1197
1948   lp: hmv (france) FALP 349
          lp: hmv (italy) QALP 10080
          lp: emi 3C153 53540-53546M/
            1C047 01400M
          cd: emi CZS 767 3592

london   hmv unpublished
8 may
1953

paris   hmv unpublished
6-11
june
1957

chopin **nocturne op 27 no 1**

london
17 october
1951

78: hmv DB 21447
45: hmv 7R 162
45: hmv (france) 7RF 265
45: hmv (italy) 7RQ 265
45: electrola 7RW 147
45: victor WHMV 1032/EHA 14
lp: victor LHMV 1032
lp: hmv (france) FALP 376
lp: emi 3C153 53540-53546M
cd: emi CZS 767 3592

paris
6-11
june
1957

hmv unpublished

nocturne op 55 no 1

london
9 october
1947

78: hmv DB 6730
lp: emi 3C153 53540-53546M
lp: discocorp RR 227
cd: emi CZS 767 3592
cd: appian APR 5571

paris
6-11
june
1957

hmv unpublished

nocturne op 55 no 2

may
1930

duo-art piano roll 7397
cd: nimbus NI 8814

london
15 october
1947

78: hmv DB 6730
lp: emi 3C153 53540-53546M
lp: discocorp RR 227
cd: emi CZS 767 3592
cd: appian APR 5571

paris
6-11
june
1957

hmv unpublished

chopin **polonaise no 1**
paris   hmv unpublished
30 april
1943

polonaise no 2
paris   hmv unpublished
30 april
1943

polonaise no 3
paris   hmv unpublished
30 april
1943

polonaise no 4
paris   hmv unpublished
30 april
1943

polonaise no 5
paris   hmv unpublished
30 april
1943

polonaise no 6
london   78: hmv DB 2014
4 july   lp: emi 3C153 53540-53546M
1933   cd: emi CZS 767 3592
                               cd: music and arts CD 717

paris   hmv unpublished
30 april
1943

tokyo   78: victor (japan) SD 3108
1-3   lp: victor (japan) JAS 273/LS 2029
december   cd: toshiba shinseido SGR 8114
1952

chopin **polonaise no 7 "polonaise-fantaisie"**
paris   hmv unpublished
30 april
1943

london   cd: music and arts CD 615
15 october   cd: appian APR 5571
1947   *unpublished hmv 78rpm recording*

chopin **prélude no 1**

hayes 22-23 march 1926	78: hmv DB 957 78: victor M 20 lp: hmv COLH 38 lp: emi 3C153 53540-53546M/ 1C047 00889M lp: discocorp RR 317 cd: emi CZS 767 3592 cd: music and arts CD 317/CD 4871
london 5 december 1927	hmv unpublished
london 4 june 1928	78: hmv DB 957 *re-recording to replace 22-23 march 1926 version*
london 11 december 1928	hmv unpublished
london 5 july 1933	78: hmv DB 2015 78: victor M 282 cd: emi CDH 761 0502 cd: philips 456 7542 *recordings in this set completed on 20 june 1934*
paris 2 december 1942	78: hmv (france) W 1541 cd: emi CZS 767 3592 cd: grammofono AB 78862 *recordings in this set completed on 25 february 1943*
london 28 june 1954	hmv unpublished
munich 11 may 1955	lp: cetra DOC 28 lp: movimento musica 01.062

chopin **prélude no 2**

hayes 22-23 march 1926	78: hmv DB 957 78: victor M 20 lp: hmv COLH 38 lp: emi 3C153 53540-53546M/ 1C047 00889M cd: music and arts CD 317/CD 4871
london 5 december 1927	78: hmv DB 958 *re-recording to replace march 1926 version*
london 4 june 1928	hmv unpublished
london 11 december 1928	hmv unpublished
london 5 july 1933	78: hmv DB 2015 78: victor M 282 cd: emi CDH 761 0502 cd: philips 456 7542 *recordings in this set completed on 20 june 1934*
paris 2 december 1942	78: hmv (france) W 1541 cd: emi CZS 767 3592 cd: grammofono AB 78862 *recordings in this set completed on 25 february 1943*
london 28 june 1954	hmv unpublished
munich 11 may 1955	lp: cetra DOC 28 lp: movimento musica 01.062

chopin **prélude no 3**

hayes 22-23 march 1926	78: hmv DB 957 78: victor M 20 lp: hmv COLH 38 lp: emi 3C153 53540-53546M/ 1C047 00889M cd: music and arts CD 317/CD 4871
london 5 december 1927	78: hmv DB 958 *re-recording to replace march 1926 version*
london 4 june 1928	hmv unpublished
london 11 december 1928	hmv unpublished
london 5 july 1933	78: hmv DB 2015 78: victor M 282 cd: emi CDH 761 0502 cd: philips 456 7542 *recordings in this set completed on 20 june 1934*
paris 2 december 1942	78: hmv (france) W 1541 cd: emi CZS 767 3592 cd: grammofono AB 78862 *recordings in this set completed on 25 february 1943*
london 28 june 1954	hmv unpublished
munich 11 may 1955	lp: cetra DOC 28 lp: movimento musica 01.062

chopin **prélude no 4**

hayes	78: hmv DB 957
22-23	78: victor M 20
march	lp: hmv COLH 38
1926	lp: emi 3C153 53540-53546M/
	1C047 00889M
	cd: music and arts CD 317/CD 4871

london	hmv unpublished
5 december	
1927	

london	78: hmv DB 957
4 june	*re-recording to replace march 1926 version*
1928	

london	hmv unpublished
11 december	
1928	

london	78: hmv DB 2015
5 july	78: victor M 282
1933	cd: emi CDH 761 0502
	cd: philips 456 7542
	recordings in this set completed on 20 june 1934

paris	78: hmv (france) W 1541
2 december	cd: emi CZS 767 3592
1942	cd: grammofono AB 78862
	recordings in this set completed on 25 february 1943

london	hmv unpublished
28 june	
1954	

munich	lp: cetra DOC 28
11 may	lp: movimento musica 01.062
1955	

chopin **prélude no 5**

hayes 22-23 march 1926	78: hmv DB 957 78: victor M 20 lp: hmv COLH 38 lp: emi 3C153 53540-53546M/ 1C047 00889M cd: music and arts CD 317/CD 4871
london 5 december 1927	78: hmv DB 958 *re-recording to replace march 1926 version*
london 4 june 1928	hmv unpublished
london 11 december 1928	hmv unpublished
london 5 july 1933	78: hmv DB 2015 78: victor M 282 cd: emi CDH 761 0502 cd: philips 456 7542 *recordings in this set completed on 20 june 1934*
paris 2 december 1942	78: hmv (france) W 1541 cd: emi CZS 767 3592 cd: grammofono AB 78862 *recordings in this set completed on 25 february 1943*
london 28 june 1954	hmv unpublished
munich 11 may 1955	lp: cetra DOC 28 lp: movimento musica 01.062

chopin **prélude no 6**

hayes	78: hmv DB 957
22-23	78: victor M 20
march	lp: hmv COLH 38
1926	lp: emi 3C153 53540-53546M/
	1C017 00889M
	cd: music and arts CD 317/CD 4871

london	hmv unpublished
5 december	
1927	

london	78: hmv DB 957
4 june	*re-recording to replace march 1926 version*
1928	

london	hmv unpublished
11 december	
1928	

london	78: hmv DB 2015
5 july	78: victor M 282
1933	cd: emi CDH 761 0502
	cd: philips 456 7542
	recordings in this set completed on 20 june 1934

paris	78: hmv (france) W 1541
2 december	cd: emi CZS 767 3592
1942	cd: grammofono AB 78862
	recordings in this set completed on 25 february 1943

london	hmv unpublished
28 june	
1954	

munich	lp: cetra DOC 28
11 may	lp: movimento musica 01.062
1955	

chopin **prélude no 7**

hayes
22-23
march
1926

78: hmv DB 958
78: victor M 20
lp: hmv COLH 38
lp: emi 3C153 53540-53546M/
        1C047 00889M
cd: music and arts CD 317/CD 4871

london
5 december
1927

78: hmv DB 958
re-recording to replace march 1926 version

london
4 june
1928

hmv unpublished

london
11 december
1928

hmv unpublished

london
5 july
1933

78: hmv DB 2016
78: victor M 282
cd: emi CDH 761 0502
cd: philips 456 7542
recordings in this set completed on 20 june 1934

paris
2 december
1942

78: hmv (france) W 1542
cd: emi CZS 767 3592
cd: grammofono AB 78862
recordings in this set completed on 25 february 1943

london
28 june
1954

hmv unpublished

munich
11 may
1955

lp: cetra DOC 28
lp: movimento musica 01.062

chopin prélude no 8

hayes 22-23 march 1926	78: hmv DB 958 78: victor M 20 lp: hmv COLH 38 lp: emi 3C153 53540-53546M/ 1C047 00889M cd: music and arts CD 317/CD 4871
london 5 december 1927	78: hmv DB 958 *re-recording to replace march 1926 version*
london 4 june 1928	hmv unpublished
london 11 december 1928	hmv unpublished
london 5 july 1933	78: hmv DB 2016 78: victor M 282 cd: emi CDH 761 0502 cd: philips 456 7542 *recordings in this set completed on 20 june 1934*
paris 2 december 1942	78: hmv (france) W 1542 cd: emi CZS 767 3592 cd: grammofono AB 78862 *recordings in this set completed on 25 february 1943*
london 28 june 1954	hmv unpublished
munich 11 may 1955	lp: cetra DOC 28 lp: movimento musica 01.062

chopin **prélude no 9**

hayes 22-23 march 1926	78: hmv DB 958 78: victor M 20 lp: hmv COLH 38 lp: emi 3C153 53540-53546M/ 1C047 00889M cd: music and arts CD 317/CD 4871
london 5 december 1927	78: hmv DB 958 *re-recording to replace march 1926 version*
london 4 june 1928	hmv unpublished
london 11 december 1928	hmv unpublished
london 5 july 1933	78: hmv DB 2016 78: victor M 282 cd: emi CDH 761 0502 cd: philips 456 7542 *recordings in this set completed on 20 june 1934*
paris 2 december 1942	78: hmv (france) W 1542 cd: emi CZS 767 3592 cd: grammofono AB 78862 *recordings in this set completed on 25 february 1943*
london 28 june 1954	hmv unpublished
munich 11 may 1955	lp: cetra DOC 28 lp: movimento musica 01.062

chopin **prélude no 10**

hayes 22-23 march 1926	78: hmv DB 958 78: victor M 20 lp: hmv COLH 38 lp: emi 3C153 53540-53546M/ 　　1C017 00889M cd: music and arts CD 317/CD 4871
london 5 december 1927	78: hmv DB 958 *re-recording to replace march 1926 version*
london 4 june 1928	hmv unpublished
london 11 december 1928	hmv unpublished
london 5 july 1933	78: hmv DB 2016 78: victor M 282 cd: emi CDH 761 0502 cd: philips 456 7542 *recordings in this set completed on 20 june 1934*
paris 2 december 1942	78: hmv (france) W 1542 cd: emi CZS 767 3592 cd: grammofono AB 78862 *recordings in this set completed on 25 february 1943*
london 28 june 1954	hmv unpublished
munich 11 may 1955	lp: cetra DOC 28 lp: movimento musica 01.062

chopin **prélude no 11**

hayes 22-23 march 1926	78: hmv DB 958 78: victor M 20 lp: hmv COLH 38 lp: emi 3C153 53540-53546M/ 1C047 00889M cd: music and arts CD 317/CD 4871
london 5 december 1927	78: hmv DB 958 *re-recording to replace march 1926 version*
london 4 june 1928	hmv unpublished
london 11 december 1928	hmv unpublished
london 5 july 1933	78: hmv DB 2016 78: victor M 282 cd: emi CDH 761 0502 cd: philips 456 7542 *recordings in this set completed on 20 june 1934*
paris 2 december 1942	78: hmv (france) W 1542 cd: emi CZS 767 3592 cd: grammofono AB 78862 *recordings in this set completed on 25 february 1943*
london 28 june 1954	hmv unpublished
munich 11 may 1955	lp: cetra DOC 28 lp: movimento musica 01.062

chopin prélude no 12

hayes 7 april 1926	78: hmv DB 958 78: victor M 20 lp: hmv COLH 38 lp: emi 3C153 53540-53546M/ 1C047 00889M cd: music and arts CD 317/CD 4871
london 5 december 1927	78: hmv DB 958 *re-recording to replace march 1926 version*
london 4 june 1928	hmv unpublished
london 11 december 1928	hmv unpublished
london 5 july 1933	78: hmv DB 2016 78: victor M 282 cd: emi CDH 761 0502 cd: philips 456 7542 *recordings in this set completed on 20 june 1934*
paris 2 december 1942	78: hmv (france) W 1542 cd: emi CZS 767 3592 cd: grammofono AB 78862 *recordings in this set completed on 25 february 1943*
munich 11 may 1955	lp: cetra DOC 28 lp: movimento musica 01.062

chopin **prélude no 13**

hayes 22-23 march 1926	78: hmv DB 958 78: victor M 20 lp: hmv COLH 38 lp: emi 3C153 53540-53546M/ 1C047 00889M cd: music and arts CD 317/CD 4871
london 5 december 1927	78: hmv DB 958 *re-recording to replace march 1926 version*
london 4 june 1928	hmv unpublished
london 11 december 1928	hmv unpublished
london 5 july 1933	78: hmv DB 2016 78: victor M 282 cd: emi CDH 761 0502 cd: philips 456 7542 *recordings in this set completed on 20 june 1934*
paris 2 december 1942	78: hmv (france) W 1542 cd: emi CZS 767 3592 cd: grammofono AB 78862 *recordings in this set completed on 25 february 1943*
london 28 june 1954	hmv unpublished
munich 11 may 1955	lp: cetra DOC 28 lp: movimento musica 01.062

chopin **prélude no 14**

hayes 22-23 march 1926	78: hmv DB 958 78: victor M 20 lp: hmv COLH 38 lp: emi 3C153 53540-53546M/ 1C017 00889M cd: music and arts CD 317/CD 4871
london 5 december 1927	78: hmv DB 958 *re-recording to replace march 1926 version*
london 4 june 1928	hmv unpublished
london 11 december 1928	hmv unpublished
london 5 july 1933	78: hmv DB 2016 78: victor M 282 cd: emi CDH 761 0502 cd: philips 456 7542 *recordings in this set completed on 20 june 1934*
paris 2 december 1942	78: hmv (france) W 1543 cd: emi CZS 767 3592 cd: grammofono AB 78862 *recordings in this set completed on 25 february 1943*
london 28 june 1954	hmv unpublished
munich 11 may 1955	lp: cetra DOC 28 lp: movimento musica 01.062

chopin **prélude no 15**

hayes 22-23 march 1926	78: hmv DB 959 78: victor M 20 lp: hmv COLH 38 lp: emi 3C153 53540-53546M/ 1C047 00889M cd: music and arts CD 317/CD 4871
london 5 december 1927	hmv unpublished
london 4 junc 1928	hmv unpublished
london 11 dccembcr 1928	hmv unpublished
london 5 july 1933	78: hmv DB 2017 78: victor M 282 cd: emi CDH 761 0502 cd: philips 456 7542 *recordings in this set completed on 20 june 1934*
paris 2 december 1942	78: hmv (france) W 1543 cd: emi CZS 767 3592 cd: grammofono AB 78862 *recordings in this set completed on 25 february 1943*
london 30 october 1950	78: hmv DB 21175
tokyo 1-3 december 1952	78: victor (japan) SD 3101 lp: victor (japan) LS 2001/RA 2087 cd: toshiba shinseido SGR 8113
london 28 june 1954	hmv unpublished
munich 11 may 1955	lp: cetra DOC 28 lp: movimcnto musica 01.062

chopin **prélude no 16**

hayes 22-23 march 1926	78: hmv DB 959 78: victor M 20 lp: hmv COLH 38 lp: emi 3C153 53540-53546M/ 1C047 00889M cd: music and arts CD 317/CD 4871
london 5 december 1927	hmv unpublished
london 4 june 1928	hmv unpublished
london 11 december 1928	hmv unpublished
london 5 july 1933	78: hmv DB 2017 78: victor M 282 cd: emi CDH 761 0502 cd: philips 456 7542 *recordings in this set completed on 20 june 1934*
paris 2 december 1942	78: hmv (france) W 1543 cd: emi CZS 767 3592 cd: grammofono AB 78862 *recordings in this set completed on 25 february 1943*
london 28 june 1954	hmv unpublished
munich 11 may 1955	lp: cetra DOC 28 lp: movimento musica 01.062

chopin **prélude no 17**

hayes	78: hmv DB 959
22-23	78: victor M 20
march	lp: hmv COLH 38
1926	lp: emi 3C153 53540-53546M/
	1C047 00889M
	cd: music and arts CD 317/CD 4871
london	hmv unpublished
5 december	
1927	
london	hmv unpublished
4 june	
1928	
london	hmv unpublished
11 december	
1928	
london	78: hmv DB 2017
5 july	78: victor M 282
1933	cd: emi CDH 761 0502
	cd: philips 456 7542
	recordings in this set completed on 20 june 1934
paris	78: hmv (france) W 1544
2 december	cd: emi CZS 767 3592
1942	cd: grammofono AB 78862
	recordings in this set completed on 25 february 1943
london	hmv unpublished
28 june	
1954	
munich	lp: cetra DOC 28
11 may	lp: movimento musica 01.062
1955	

chopin **prélude no 18**

hayes 22-23 march 1926	78: hmv DB 959 78: victor M 20 lp: hmv COLH 38 lp: emi 3C153 53540-53546M/ 1C047 00889M cd: music and arts CD 317/CD 4871
london 5 december 1927	hmv unpublished
london 4 june 1928	hmv unpublished
london 11 december 1928	hmv unpublished
london 5 july 1933	78: hmv DB 2017 78: victor M 282 cd: emi CDH 761 0502 cd: philips 456 7542 *recordings in this set completed on 20 june 1934*
paris 2 december 1942	78: hmv (france) W 1544 cd: emi CZS 767 3592 cd: grammofono AB 78862 *recordings in this set completed on 25 february 1943*
london 28 june 1954	hmv unpublished
munich 11 may 1955	lp: cetra DOC 28 lp: movimento musica 01.062

chopin **prélude no 19**

hayes	78: hmv DB 960
22-23	78: victor M 20
march	lp: hmv COLH 38
1926	lp: emi 3C153 53540-53546M/
	1C047 00889M
	cd: music and arts CD 317/CD 4871

london	hmv unpublished
5 december	
1927	

london	78: hmv DB 960
4 june	*re-recording to replace march 1926 version*
1928	

london	hmv unpublished
11 december	
1928	

london	78: hmv DB 2018
5 july	78: victor M 282
1933	cd: emi CDH 761 0502
	cd: philips 456 7542
	recordings in this set completed on 20 june 1934

paris	78: hmv (france) W 1544
2 december	cd: emi CZS 767 3592
1942	cd: grammofono AB 78862
	recordings in this set completed on 25 february 1943

london	hmv unpublished
28 june	
1954	

munich	lp: cetra DOC 28
11 may	lp: movimento musica 01.062
1955	

chopin **prélude no 20**

hayes 22-23 march 1926	78: hmv DB 960 78: victor M 20 lp: hmv COLH 38 lp: emi 3C153 53540-53546M/ 1C017 00889M cd: music and arts CD 317/CD 4871
london 5 december 1927	hmv unpublished
london 4 june 1928	78: hmv DB 960 *re-recording to replace march 1926 version*
london 11 december 1928	hmv unpublished
london 5 july 1933	78: hmv DB 2018 78: victor M 282 cd: emi CDH 761 0502 cd: philips 456 7542 *recordings in this set completed on 20 june 1934*
paris 2 december 1942	78: hmv (france) W 1544 cd: emi CZS 767 3592 cd: grammofono AB 78862 *recordings in this set completed on 25 february 1943*
london 28 june 1954	hmv unpublished
munich 11 may 1955	lp: cetra DOC 28 lp: movimento musica 01.062

chopin **prélude no 21**

hayes 22-23 march 1926	78: hmv DB 960 78: victor M 20 lp: hmv COLH 38 lp: emi 3C153 53540-53546M/ 1C047 00889M cd: music and arts CD 317/CD 4871
london 5 december 1927	hmv unpublished
london 4 june 1928	78: hmv DB 960 *re-recording to replace march 1926 version*
london 11 december 1928	hmv unpublished
london 5 july 1933	78: hmv DB 2018 78: victor M 282 cd: emi CDH 761 0502 cd: philips 456 7542 *recordings in this set completed on 20 june 1934*
paris 2 december 1942	78: hmv (france) W 1544 cd: emi CZS 767 3592 cd: grammofono AB 78862 *recordings in this set completed on 25 february 1943*
london 28 june 1954	hmv unpublished
munich 11 may 1955	lp: cetra DOC 28 lp: movimento musica 01.062

chopin **prélude no 22**

hayes 22-23 march 1926	78: hmv DB 960 78: victor M 20 lp: hmv COLH 38 lp: emi 3C153 53540-53546M/ 1C047 00889M cd: music and arts CD 317/CD 4871
london 5 december 1927	hmv unpublished
london 4 june 1928	78: hmv DB 960 *re-recording to replace march 1926 version*
london 11 december 1928	hmv unpublished
london 5 july 1933	78: hmv DB 2018 78: victor M 282 cd: emi CDH 761 0502 cd: philips 456 7542 *recordings in this set completed on 20 june 1934*
paris 2 december 1942	78: hmv (france) W 1544 cd: emi CZS 767 3592 cd: grammofono AB 78862 *recordings in this set completed on 25 february 1943*
london 28 june 1954	hmv unpublished
munich 11 may 1955	lp: cetra DOC 28 lp: movimento musica 01.062

chopin **prélude no 23**

hayes	78: hmv DB 960
22-23	78: victor M 20
march	lp: hmv COLH 38
1926	lp: emi 3C153 53540-53546M/
	1C047 00889M
	cd: music and arts CD 317/CD 4871

london	hmv unpublished
5 december	
1927	

london	78: hmv DB 960
4 june	*re-recording to replace march 1926 version*
1928	

london	hmv unpublished
11 december	
1928	

london	78: hmv DB 2018
5 july	78: victor M 282
1933	cd: emi CDH 761 0502
	cd: philips 456 7542
	recordings in this set completed on 20 june 1934

paris	78: hmv (france) W 1544
2 december	cd: emi CZS 767 3592
1942	cd: grammofono AB 78862
	recordings in this set completed on 25 february 1943

london	hmv unpublished
28 june	
1954	

munich	lp: cetra DOC 28
11 may	lp: movimento musica 01.062
1955	

chopin **prélude no 24**

hayes 22-23 march 1926	78: hmv DB 960 78: victor M 20 lp: hmv COLH 38 lp: emi 3C153 53540-53546M/ 1C047 00889M cd: music and arts CD 317/CD 4871
london 5 december 1927	hmv unpublished
london 4 june 1928	78: hmv DB 960 *re-recording to replace march 1926 version*
london 11 december 1928	hmv unpublished
london 5 july 1933	78: hmv DB 2018 78: victor M 282 cd: emi CDH 761 0502 cd: philips 456 7542 *recordings in this set completed on 20 june 1934*
paris 2 december 1942	78: hmv (france) W 1544 cd: emi CZS 767 3592 cd: grammofono AB 78862 *recordings in this set completed on 25 february 1943*
london 28 june 1954	hmv unpublished
munich 11 may 1955	lp: cetra DOC 28 lp: movimento musica 01.062

complete set of 24 préludes recorded in munich in 1955 also issued on cd by foyer CDS 16003

chopin **prélude no 25**

london	cd: music and arts CD 617
10 october	cd: appian APR 5571
1947	*unpublished hmv 78rpm recording*

london	78: hmv DB 21018
4 november	45: hmv (france) 7RF 239
1949	lp: hmv COLH 38
	lp: emi 3C153 53540-53546M/
	1C047 00889M
	lp: world records SH 327
	cd: emi CDH 761 0502/CZS 767 3592
	cd: music and arts CD 317

scherzo no 1

paris	hmv unpublished
14 april	
1943	

scherzo no 2

london	hmv unpublished
19 may	
1937	

paris	hmv unpublished
14 april	
1943	

tokyo	78: victor (japan) SD 3110
1-3	lp: victor (japan) LS 2029
december	cd: toshiba shinseido SGR 8114
1952	

scherzo no 3

paris	hmv unpublished
14 april	
1943	

tokyo	78: victor (japan) SD 3110
1-3	lp: victor (japan) LS 2029
december	cd: toshiba shinseido SGR 8114
1952	

chopin **scherzo no 4**
paris   hmv unpublished
14 april
1943

tarantelle in a flat
camden nj   78: victor 561/64910
29 january   78: hmv DA 145
1920   cd: biddulph LHW 014-015

camden nj   78: victor 561/64910
27 february   cd: biddulph LHW 014-015
1923   *re-recording to replace 29 january 1920 version*

london   78: hmv DA 1213
13 may
1931

london   78: hmv DB 2032
5 july   78: victor 8251
1933   lp: emi 3C153 53540-53546M
                                           cd: emi CZS 767 3592

paris   hmv unpublished
14 september
1943

london   78: hmv DA 2071
8 may   lp: hmv ALP 1197
1953   lp: hmv (france) FALP 349
                                           lp: hmv (italy) QALP 10080
                                           lp: emi 1C047 01400M
                                           although this was a ten-inch 78rpm recording,
                                           a twelve-inch matrix was also made but not used

london   78: hmv DB 21492
22 july
1954

chopin **scherzo no 4**
paris   hmv unpublished
14 april
1943

tarantclle in a flat
camden nj   78: victor 561/64910
29 january   78: hmv DA 145
1920   cd: biddulph LHW 014-015

camden nj   78: victor 561/64910
27 february   cd: biddulph LHW 014-015
1923   *re-recording to replace 29 january 1920 version*

london   78: hmv DA 1213
13 may
1931

london   78: hmv DB 2032
5 july   78: victor 8251
1933   lp: emi 3C153 53540-53546M
                                       cd: emi CZS 767 3592

paris   hmv unpublished
14 september
1943

london   78: hmv DA 2071
8 may   lp: hmv ALP 1197
1953   lp: hmv (france) FALP 349
                                       lp: hmv (italy) QALP 10080
                                       lp: cmi 1C047 01400M
                                       although this was a ten-inch 78rpm recording,
                                       a twelve-inch matrix was also made but not used

london   78: hmv DB 21492
22 july
1954

chopin **valse op 18**
london
19-20
june
1934

78: hmv DB 2311
78: victor M 229
lp: hmv COLH 32
lp: emi 3C153 53540-53546M
cd: cmi CZS 767 3592

paris
24 may
1943

78: hmv (france) W 1604
cd: cmi CZS 767 3592

valse op 34 no 1
london
19 20
june
1934

78: hmv DB 2311
78: victor M 229
lp: hmv COLH 32
lp: cmi 3C153 53540-53546M

paris
24 may
1943

78: hmv (france) W 1603
cd: cmi CZS 767 3592

valse op 34 no 2
london
19-20
june
1934

78: hmv DB 2312
78: victor M 229
lp: hmv COLH 32
lp: cmi 3C153 53540-53546M

paris
24 may
1943

78: hmv (france) W 1603
cd: cmi CZS 767 3592

london
16 october
1951

hmv unpublished

chopin **valse op 34 no 3**

london | 78: hmv DB 2312
19-20 | 78: victor M 229
june | lp: hmv COLH 32
1934 | lp: emi 3C153 53540-53546M

paris | 78: hmv (france) DA 4962
24 may | cd: cmi CZS 767 3592
1943

valse op 42

london | 78: hmv DB 2313
19 20 | 78: victor M 229
june | lp: hmv COLH 32
1934 | lp: cmi 3C153 53540-53546M
| cd: emi CZS 767 3592

paris | 78: hmv (france) W 1605
24 may | cd: emi CZS 767 3592
1943

chopin **valse op 64 no 1**

london	78: hmv DB 2313
19-20	78: victor M 229
june	lp: hmv COLH 32
1934	lp: emi 3C153 53540-53546M
paris	78: hmv (france) W 1605
24 may	cd: emi CZS 767 3592
1943	
london	78: hmv DB 21070
14 november	45: victor WHMV 1032
1949	lp: hmv ALP 1197
	lp: victor LHMV 1032
london	hmv unpublished
30 october	
1950	
london	hmv unpublished
16 october	
1951	
tokyo	78: victor (japan) SD 3101
1-3	lp: victor (japan) LS 2001/RA 2087
december	
1952	

chopin **valse op 64 no 2**

camden nj	78: victor 1101
21 march	78: hmv DB 1321
1925	cd: piano library PL 214
	cd: biddulph LHW 020
	cd: emi CZS 767 3592
	cd: asv CDAJA 5112
london	78: hmv DB 1321
13 march	lp: discocorp RR 227
1929	cd: biddulph LHW 014-015
london	78: hmv DB 2314
19-20	78: victor M 229
june	lp: hmv COLH 32
1934	lp: emi 3C153 53540-53546M
paris	78: hmv (france) DA 4962
24 may	cd: emi CZS 767 3592
1943	
london	hmv unpublished
30 october	
1950	
london	78: hmv DA 2071
8 may	45: victor WHMV 1032
1953	lp: hmv ALP 1197
	lp: victor LHMV 1032

chopin **valse op 64 no 3**

london	78: hmv DB 2314
19-20	78: victor M 229
june	lp: hmv COLH 32
1934	lp: emi 3C153 53540-53546M

paris	78: hmv (france) DA 4963
24 may	cd: emi CZS 767 3592
1943	

valse op 69 no 1

london	78: hmv DB 2315
19 20	78: victor M 229
june	lp: hmv COLH 32
1934	lp: emi 3C153 53540-53546M

london	78: hmv DA 1213
13 may	
1931	

paris	78: hmv (france) DA 4963
24 may	cd: emi CZS 767 3592
1943	

paris	vhs video: warner/nvc 3984 291993
1944	dvd video: warner/nvc 3984 291992

london	78: hmv DB 21094
4 november	45: victor WHMV 1032
1949	lp: hmv ALP 1197
	lp: victor LHMV 1032

london	hmv unpublished
16 october	
1951	

chopin **valse op 69 no 2**

london	78: hmv DB 2315
19-20	78: victor M 229
june	lp: hmv COLH 32
1934	lp: emi 3C153 53540-53546M
	cd: cmi CZS 767 3592

paris	78: hmv (france) W 1604
24 may	cd: cmi CZS 767 3592
1943	

valse op 70 no 1

london	78: hmv DB 2316
19 20	78: victor M 229
june	lp: hmv COLH 32
1934	lp: cmi 3C153 53540-53546M

paris	78: hmv (france) DA 4964
24 may	cd: cmi CZS 767 3592
1943	

london	78: hmv DB 21094
4 november	45: victor WHMV 1032
1949	lp: hmv ALP 1197
	lp: victor LHMV 1032

tokyo	78: victor (japan) SF 727
1-3	45: victor (japan) EP 3042
december	cd: venezia (japan) V 1003
1952	

chopin **valse op 70 no 2**
london
19-20
june
1934

78: hmv DB 2313
78: victor M 229
lp: hmv COLH 32
lp: emi 3C153 53540-53546M

paris
24 may
1943

78: hmv (france) W 1605
cd: emi CZS 767 3592

london
16 october
1951

45: victor WHMV 1032
lp: victor LHMV 1032

valse op 70 no 3
london
19-20
june
1934

78: hmv DB 2316
78: victor M 229
lp: hmv COLH 32
lp: emi 3C153 53540-53546M

paris
24 may
1943

78: hmv (france) W 1604
cd: emi CZS 767 3592

valse in e minor op posth
london
19-20
june
1934

78: hmv DB 2316
78: victor M 229
lp: hmv COLH 32
lp: emi 3C153 53540-53546M
cd: emi CZS 767 3592

paris
24 may
1943

78: hmv (france) DA 4694
cd: emi CZS 767 3592

FRANCOIS COUPERIN (1668-1733)

concert dans le gout théatrale, arranged by cortot

paris	école normale	78: hmv DB 1767-1768
3 december	chamber	
1931	orchestra	
	cortot conducts	

CLAUDE DEBUSSY (1863-1918)

children's corner (doctor gradus ad parnassum; jimbo's lullaby; serenade for a doll; the snow is dancing; the little shepherd; golliwog's cakewalk)

hayes	78: hmv DB 678-679
5 december	cd: biddulph LHW 021
1923	

london	hmv unpublished
5 december	
1927	

london	78: hmv DB 1248-1249
5 june	78: victor 7147-7148
1928	cd: biddulph LHW 006
	cd: dante HPC 089-090
	recording completed on 11 december 1928

london	78: hmv DB 6725-6726
10 october	45: victor ERA 9137
1947	lp: hmv (italy) QALP 10127
	cd: appian APR 5571

london	hmv unpublished
7-8	
may	
1953	

golliwog's cakewalk/children's corner

tokyo	78: victor (japan) SF 728
1-3	lp: victor (japan) LS 105
december	cd: toshiba shinseido SGR 8114
1952	

debussy **danseuses de delphes/préludes livre 1**

london 78: hmv DA 1240
12 may 78: victor M 149
1931 45: victor WHMV 1009
cd: biddulph LHW 006
cd: dante HPC 089-090
cd: philips 456 7542
earlier session held in paris in 1930

london 78: hmv DB 9578-9582
24 october 78: victor M 480
1949 45: victor WHMV 1009
lp: hmv BLP 1006
lp: hmv (france) FALP 360
lp: hmv (italy) QBLP 5020
lp: victor LHMV 1009

voiles/préludes livre 1

london 78: hmv DA 1240
12 may 78: victor M 149
1931 cd: biddulph LHW 006
cd: dante HPC 089-090
cd: philips 456 7542
earlier session held in paris in 1930

london 78: hmv DB 9578-9582
24 october 78: victor M 480
1949 45: victor WHMV 1009
lp: hmv BLP 1006
lp: hmv (france) FALP 360
lp: hmv (italy) QBLP 5020
lp: victor LHMV 1009

dcbussy **le vent dans la pleine/préludes livre 1**

london	78: hmv DB 1249
5 june	78: victor 7148
1928	cd: biddulph LHW 006
	cd: dante HPC 089-090

london	78: hmv DA 1241
12 may	78: victor M 149
1931	cd: biddulph LHW 006
	cd: dante HPC 089-090
	cd: philips 456 7542
	earlier session held in paris in 1930

london	78: hmv DB 9578-9582
24 october	78: victor M 480
1949	45: victor WHMV 1009
	lp: hmv BLP 1006
	lp: hmv (france) FALP 360
	lp: hmv (italy) QBLP 5020
	lp: victor LHMV 1009

les sons et les parfums tournent dans l'air du soir/préludes livre 1

london	78: hmv DA 1241
12 may	78: victor M 149
1931	cd: biddulph LHW 006
	cd: dante HPC 089-090
	cd: philips 456 7542
	earlier session held in paris in 1930

london	78: hmv DB 9578-9582
24 october	78: victor M 480
1949	45: victor WHMV 1009
	lp: hmv BLP 1006
	lp: hmv (france) FALP 360
	lp: hmv (italy) QBLP 5020
	lp: victor LHMV 1009

dcbussy **les collines d'anacapri/préludes livre 1**

london	78: hmv DA 1242
12 may	78: victor M 149
1931	cd: biddulph LHW 006
	cd: dante HPC 098-090
	cd: philips 156 7542
	earlier session held in paris in 1930

london	78: hmv DB 9578-9582
24 october	78: victor M 480
1949	45: victor WHMV 1009
	lp: hmv BLP 1006
	lp: hmv (francc) FALP 360
	lp: hmv (italy) QBLP 5020
	lp: victor LHMV 1009

des pas sur la neige/préludes livre 1

london	78: hmv DA 1242
12 may	78: victor M 149
1931	cd: bidulph LHW 006
	cd: dante HPC 089-090
	cd: philips 456 7542
	earlier session held in paris in 1930

london	78: hmv DB 9578-9582
24 octobcr	78: victor M 480
1949	45: victor WHMV 1009/EHA 3
	lp: hmv BLP 1006
	lp: hmv (france) FALP 360
	lp: hmv (italy) QBLP 5020
	lp: victor LHMV 1009

ce qu'a vu le vent d'ouest/préludes livre 1

london	78: hmv·DA 1243
12 may	78: victor M 149
1931	cd: biddulph LHW 006
	cd: dante HPC 089-090
	cd: philips 456 7542
	earlier session held in paris in 1930

london	78: victor DB 9578-9582
24 october	78: victor M 480
1949	45: victor WHMV 1009/EHA 3
	lp: hmv BLP 1006
	lp: hmv (france) FALP 360
	lp: hmv (italy) QBLP 5020
	lp: victor LHMV 1009

dcbussy **la fille aux cheveux de lin/préludes livre 1**

8 january	78: victor 562/64956
1919	78: hmv DA 146
	cd: piano library PL 214
	cd: pearl GEMMCD 9386
	cd: biddulph LHW 014-015

london	78: hmv DB 1249
5 junc	78: victor 7148
1928	cd: biddulph LHW 006
	cd: dante HPC 089-090

london	78: hmv DA 1243
12 may	78: victor M 149
1931	cd: biddulph LHW 006
	cd: dante HPC 089-090
	cd: philips 456 7542
	earlier session held in paris in 1930

london	78: hmv DB 9578-9782
24 octobcr	78: victor M 480
1949	45: victor WHMV 1009/EHA 3
	lp: hmv BLP 1006
	lp: hmv (france) FALP 360
	lp: hmv (italy) QBLP 5020
	lp: victor LHMV 1009

la sérénade interrompue/préludes livre 1

london	78: hmv DA 1244
12 may	78: victor M 149
1931	cd: biddulph LHW 006
	cd: dante HPC 089-090
	cd: philips 456 7542
	earlier session held in paris in 1930

london	78: hmv DB 9578-9582
24 october	78: victor M 480
1949	45: victor WHMV 1009/EHA 3
	lp: hmv BLP 1006
	lp: hmv (france) FALP 360
	lp: hmv (italy) QBLP 5020
	lp: victor LHMV 1009

debussy **la cathédrale engloutie/préludes livre 1**

hayes	78: hmv DA 679
october	cd: biddilph LHW 003/LHW 021
1923	cd: dante HPC 089-090
london	hmv unpublished
5 december	
1927	
paris	78: hmv DB 1593
2 june	78: victor M 149
1930	cd: biddulph LHW 006
	cd: dante HPC 089-090
	cd: philips 456 7542
london	78: hmv DB 6726
14 october	cd: appian APR 5571
1947	
london	78: hmv DB 9578-9582
24 october	78: victor M 480
1949	45: victor WHMV 1009/EHA 3
	lp: hmv BLP 1006
	lp: hmv (france) FALP 360
	lp: hmv (italy) QBLP 5020
	lp: victor LHMV 1009

debussy **la danse de puck/préludes livre 1**

paris	78: hmv DB 1593
2 june	78: victor M 149
1930	cd: biddulph LHW 006
	cd: dante HPC 089-090
	cd: philips 456 7512
london	78: hmv DB 9578-9582
24 october	78: victor M 480
1949	45: victor WHMV 1009
	lp: hmv BLP 1006
	lp: hmv (france) FALP 360
	lp: hmv (italy) QBLP 5020
	lp: victor LHMV 1009

debussy **minstrels/préludes livre 1**

camden nj	cd: pearl GEMMCD 9386
8 january	cd: biddulph LHW 014-015
1919	*unpublished victor 78rpm recording*

london	78: hmv DA 1244
12 may	78: victor M 149
1931	cd: biddulph LHW 006
	cd: dante HPC 089-090
	cd: philips 456 7542
	earlier session held in paris in 1930

london	78: hmv DB 9578-9582
24 october	78: victor M 480
1949	45: victor WHMV 1009
	lp: hmv BLP 1006
	lp: hmv (france) FALP 360
	lp: hmv (italy) QBLP 5020
	lp: victor LHMV 1009

minstrels/préludes livre 1, arranged by hartmann for violin and piano

paris	thibaud, violin	78: hmv DB 1323
7 june		78: victor 8184
1929		cd: biddulph LHW 006
		cd: emi CDH 763 0322
		cd: dante HPC 013/HPC 089-090
		cd: appian APR 7028
		cd: music memoria MM 30321

violin sonata

paris	thibaud, violin	78: hmv DB 1322-1323
7 june		78: victor 8183-8184
1929		cd: biddulph LHW 006
		cd: emi CDH 763 0322
		cd: music memoria MM 30321
		cd: pearl GEMMCD 9348
		cd: dante HPC 089-090

dcbussy ballade des femmes de paris/3 ballades de francois villon

london	teyte, soprano	78: hmv DA 1477
13 march		78: victor M 322
1936		lp: hmv COLH 134
		lp: emi EX 29 04021
		cd: cmi CHS 761 0382
		cd: pearl GEMMCD 9134
		cd: dantc HPC 089-090

3 chansons de bilitis (la flute de pan; la chevelure; le tombeau des naides)

london	teyte, soprano	78: hmv DA 1474-1475
12-13		78: victor M 322
march		lp: hmv COLH 134
1936		lp: emi EX 29 04021
		cd: emi CHS 761 0382
		cd: pearl GEMMCD 9134
		cd: dante HPC 089-090

debussy **de greve/proses lyriques**

london	teyte, soprano	78: hmv DA 1477
13 march		78: victor M 322
1936		lp: hmv COLH 134
		lp: emi EX 29 04021
		cd: emi CHS 761 0382
		cd: pearl GEMMCD 9134
		cd: dante HPC 089-090
		cd: dutton CDBP 9724

fetes galantes (les ingénus; en sourdine; fantoches; le faune; colloque sentimental; clair de lune)

london	teyte, soprano	78: hmv DA 1471-1473
12 march		78: victor M 322
1936		lp: hmv COLH 134
		lp: emi EX 29 04021
		cd: emi CHS 761 0382
		cd: pearl GEMMCD 9134
		cd: dante HPC 089-090

le promenoir des amants (aupres de cette grotte sombre; crois mon conseil; je tremble en voyant son visage)

london	teyte, soprano	78: hmv DA 1474-1475
12-13		78: victor M 322
march		lp: hmv COLH 134
1936		lp: emi EX 29 04021
		cd: emi CHS 761 0382
		cd: pearl GEMMCD 9134
		cd: dante HPC 089-090

GABRIEL FAURE (1845-1924)

violin sonata no 1

hayes	thibaud, violin	hmv unpublished
22 october		*recording incomplete: recording of allegro vivo*
1923		*movement only completed on 24 october 1923*
		and 11 november 1924

london	thibaud, violin	78: hmv DB 1080-1082
23 june		78: victor 8086-8088
1927		lp: hmv COLH 74
		lp: angel GR 70010
		lp: discocorp RR 528
		cd: emi CDH 763 0322
		cd: symposium SYMCD 1156
		cd: biddulph LAB 116
		cd: malibran CDRG 150

berceuse for violin and piano

paris	thibaud, violin	78: hmv DB 1653
2 july		78: victor M 165
1931		lp: toshiba GR 2133
		lp: emi 2C051 03719
		cd: emi CDH 763 0322
		cd: biddulph LAB 029/LAB 116
		cd: appian APR 7028

berceuse from dolly suite for piano duet, arranged for solo piano by cortot

1925	duo-art piano roll
	lp: decca SDDR 173
	cd: biddulph LHW 014-015

les berceaux/3 mélodies op 23

paris	litvinne, soprano	g & t 33159
22 december		cd: symposium SYMCD 1101
1902		*subsequently re-recorded with another pianist*

CESAR FRANCK (1822-1890)

variations symphoniques pour piano et orchestre

london	london	78: hmv DB 1069-1070
22 june	symphony	78: victor 6734-6735
1927	ronald	cd: music and arts CD 718

london	orchestra	hmv unpublished
11 march	ronald	
1932		

london	london	78: hmv DB 2185-2186
12-13	philharmonic	78: victor 8357-8358
march	ronald	lp: hmv COLH 31
1934		cd: biddulph LHW 027
		cd: philips 456 7542
		cd: dante HPC 010
		cd: naxos 811.0613

prélude, aria et final

london	78: hmv DB 1695-1697
8 march	78: victor M 163
1932	lp: toshiba GR 2031
	cd: biddulph LHW 027
	cd: philips 456 7542
	cd: dante HPC 010

london	hmv unpublished
14 october	
1947	

franck prélude, chorale et fugue

london		78: hmv DB 1299-1300
6 march		78: victor 7331-7332
1929		cd: biddulph LHW 027
		cd: philips 456 7542
		cd: dante HPC 010
		recording completed on 19 march 1929

paris		hmv unpublished
19 may		
1930		

london		hmv unpublished
24-25		*recording completed on 30 october 1950*
october		
1950		

violin sonata in a

hayes	thibaud, violin	78: hmv DB 785-788
22-24		78: victor 6524-6527
october		cd: biddulph LAB 014
1923		*recording completed on 11 november 1924*

paris	thibaud, violin	78: hmv DB 1347-1350
28 may		78: victor M 81
1929		lp: discocorp RR 528
		lp: toshiba GR 2024
		cd: emi CDH 763 0322
		cd: biddulph LHW 027

piano quintet in f minor

london	international	78: hmv DB 1099-1102
12 december	string quartet	78: victor M 38
1927		lp: discocorp RR 463
		cd: biddulph LHW 029
		cd: dante HPC 010

CHARLES GOUNOD (1818-1893)

seigneur daignez permettre/faust

paris	litvinne, soprano	g& t 33001
1903		cd: symposium SYMCD 1151

o ma lyre immortelle/sapho

paris	litvinne, soprano	g& t 33000
1903		

GEORGE FRIDERIC HANDEL (1685-1759)

air and variations from suite no 5 "harmonious blacksmith"

camden nj	78: victor 6752
27 october	78: hmv DB 1145
1926	cd: biddulph LHW 020

FRANZ JOSEF HAYDN (1732-1809)

piano trio no 25 in g

london	thibaud, violin	78: hmv DA 895-896
6 june	casals, cello	78: victor 3045-3046
1927		lp: hmv COLH 12
		lp: emi HLM 7017/1C047 01148M/ 3C161 50089-50091M
		cd: emi CHS 764 0572
		cd: biddulph LAB 028
		cd: naxos 811.0188
		presto only
		cd: beulah 1PD 4

FRANZ LISZT (1811-1886)

piano sonata in b minor

london	78: hmv DB 1307-1309
13 march	78: victor 7325-7327
1929	lp: emi 1C047 01504M
	lp: angel 60241
	cd: music and arts CD 622/CD 4622
	cd: pearl GEMMCD 9396

la leggierezza/3 études de concert

camden nj	78: victor 74589/6065
8 january	78: hmv DB 643
1919	cd: music and arts CD 615/CD 622/
	CD 4622
	cd: pearl GEMMCD 9396
	cd: biddulph LHW 014-015

london	78: hmv DB 1535
13 may	cd: music and arts CD 622/CD 4622
1930	cd: pearl GEMMCD 9491

paris	hmv unpublished
21 may	
1930	

saint francois marchant sur les flots

london	78: hmv DB 3269
19 may	78: victor 15245
1937	cd: music and arts CD 615
	cd: pearl GEMMCD 9396/GEMMCD 9491

liszt **au bord d'une source/années de pelerinage**

camden nj	78: victor 982/66213
2 january	78: hmv DA 609
1923	cd: music and arts CD 615
	cd: pearl GEMMCD 9396
	cd: biddulph LHW 014-015

october	duo-art piano roll 6663
1923	cd: nimbus NI 8814

la campanella/études d'exécution transcendante

hayes	hmv unpublished
21 march	
1925	

hungarian rhapsody no 2 in s sharp minor

camden nj	78: victor 6335/74670
28 january	cd: pearl GEMMCD 9396
1920	cd: biddulph LHW 014-015

camden nj	78: victor 74670 and 74822
1 march	cd: biddulph LHW 014-015
1923	

camden nj	78: victor 6626 and 6810
27-28	cd: music and arts CD 615
december	cd: philips 456 7512
1926	

may	duo-art piano roll 3099
1927	cd: nimbus NI 8814

tokyo	78: victor (japan) SD 3103
1-3	lp: victor (japan) LS 105
december	cd: toshiba shinseido SGR 8114
1952	

liszt hungarian rhapsody no 11 in a minor

camden nj	cd: pearl GEMMCD 9396
21 march	*unpublished victor 78rpm recording*
1925	

camden nj	78: victor 1277
27 october	78: hmv DA 952
1926	cd: pearl GEMMCD 9491
	cd: music and arts CD 615
	cd: philips 456 7512
	recording completed on 27 december 1926

| january | duo art piano roll 6135 |
| 1927 | cd: nimbus NI 8814 |

tokyo	78: victor (japan) SD 3104
1-3	lp: victor (japan) LS 105
december	cd: toshiba shinseido SGR 8114
1952	

london	78: hmv DB 21618
9 may	45: hmv 7R 174
1953	

JACQUES THIBAUD

PABLO CASALS

CORTOT

"His Master's Voice"

—MID-MARCH—1930

FELIX MENDELSSOHN-BARTHOLDY (1809-1847)

variations sérieuses in d minor

london	78: hmv DB 3266-3267
19 may	78: victor 15173-15174
1937	cd: biddulph LHW 002

london	78: hmv DA 7042-7043
24 october 1950	*recording completed on 30 october 1950*

tokyo	78: victor (japan) SD 3105
1-3 december	
1952	

sweet remembrance/lieder ohne worte

london	78: hmv DB 3267
19 may	78: victor 15174
1937	cd: biddulph LHW 002

rondo capriccioso in e

camden nj	78: victor 6358/74810
6 february 1923	cd: biddulph LHW 014-015

scherzo in e/3 fantasies op 16

camden nj	78: victor 66261
5 february	lp: toshiba GR 70007
1923	cd: biddulph LHW 014-015

piano trio no 1

london	thibaud, violin	78: hmv DB 1072-1075
20-21	casals, cello	78: victor M 126
june		lp: emi HLM 7105/1C049 01808M/
1927		RLS 723/1C153 52475-52477M
		cd: emi CHS 764 0572
		cd: biddulph LAB 028/LHW 002
		cd: monopoly GI 20059

scherzo/piano trio no 2

london	thibaud, violin	hmv unpublished
6 july 1926	casals, cello	

EDUARD NAPRAVNIK (1839-1916)

berceuse d'harold

paris	litvinne, soprano	g & t 33161
29 december		cd: symposium SYMCD 1101
1902		*subsequently re-recorded with another pianist*

HENRY PURCELL (1659-1695)

minuets in g and f, arranged by henderson

london	78: hmv DA 1609
26 october	lp: toshiba GR 2211
1937	cd: biddulph LHW 020

london	78: hmv DA 1901
19 april	lp: hmv ALP 1197
1948	lp: toshiba GR 2218

air in g, gavotte in g and sicilienne in g minor, arranged by henderson

london	78: hmv DA 1609
26 october	lp: toshiba GR 2211
1937	cd: biddulph LHW 020

MAURICE RAVEL (1875-1937)

piano concerto for the left hand

paris	conservatoire	78: hmv DB 3885-3886
12 may	orchestra	78: victor M 629
1939	münch	lp: angel GR 2112
		cd: emi CDH 565 4992
		cd: pearl GEMMCD 9491
		cd: naxos 811.0613

gaspard de la nuit

london	hmv unpublished
10 march	*damaged matrix*
1939	

sonatine

paris	hmv unpublished
21 may	
1930	

london	78: hmv DB 1533-1534
11 may	78: victor 7728-7729
1931	lp: emi HQM 1182
	cd: philips 456 7542

jeux d'eau

camden nj	78: victor 6065/74659
28 january	78: hmv DB 643
1920	cd: biddulph LHW 014-015
	cd: pearl GEMMCD 9386
	cd: piano library PL 214

camden nj	78: victor 6065/74659
1 march	cd: biddulph LHW 014-015
1923	*re-recording to replace 28 january 1920 version*

london	78: hmv DB 1534
11 may	78: victor 7729
1931	lp: emi HQM 1182
	cd: philips 456 7542

ANTON RUBINSTEIN (1829-1894)

night

paris	litvinne, soprano	g & t 23196
29 december		
1902		

CAMILLE SAINT-SAENS (1835-1921)

piano concerto no 4

london	orchestra	78: hmv DB 2577-2579
9 july	münch	78: victor M 367
1935		lp: rococo 2040
		cd: pearl GEMMCD 9491
		cd: dante LYS 306
		cd: philips 456 7542
		cd: naxos 811.0613

bourrée for the left hand

camden nj	78: victor 1016/66262
1 march	cd: pearl GEMMCD 9386
1923	cd: biddulph LHW 014-015

tokyo	78: victor (japan) SF 728
1-3	lp: victor (japan) LS 105
december	cd: toshiba shinseido SGR 8114
1952	

saint-saens **étude en forme de valse**

camden nj	78: victor 6063/74588
9 january	78: hmv DB 167
1919	cd: music and arts CD 615
	cd: piano library PL 214
	cd: pearl GEMMCD 9386
	cd: biddulph LHW 014-015
december	duo-art piano roll 6732
1920	lp: decca SDDR 173
	cd: nimbus NI 8814
paris	hmv unpublished
21 may	
1930	
london	78: hmv DB 1535
13 may	cd: pearl GEMMCD 9396/GEMMCD 9491
1931	cd: biddulph LHW 020
	cd: dante HPC 089-090
	cd: naxos 811.0613

samson et dalila, excerpt (mon coeur s'ouvre a ta voix)

paris	litvinne, soprano	g & t 33160
29 december		cd: symposium SYMCD 1101
1902		*subsequently re-recorded with another pianist*

FRANZ SCHUBERT (1797-1828)

moment musical no 3 in f minor

london
1952

lp: hmv ALP 1197
lp: hmv (france) FALP 349
lp: hmv (italy) QALP 10080

tokyo
1-3
december
1952

78: victor (japan) M 335
lp: victor (japan) LS 105
cd: toshiba shinseido SGR 8114

impromptu d935 no 3

december
1920

duo-art piano roll
lp: decca SDDR 173

12 ländler d790

london
19 may
1937

78: hmv DB 3268
cd: biddulph LHW 020

london
17 october
1951

78: hmv DB 21492
lp: emi 1C047 01400

schubert litanei auf das fest allerseelen, song arranged for solo piano by liszt and cortot

1920   duo-art piano roll
                                 lp: decca SDDR 173

camden nj   78: victor 6502
21 march   cd: pearl GEMMCD 9386
1925   cd: piano library PL 214
                                 cd: biddulph LHW 014-015

london   hmv unpublished
6 december
1927

london   78: hmv DB 3338
19 may   78: victor 14612
1937   cd: biddulph LHW 020

london   78: hmv DA 1898
19 april
1948

tokyo   78: victor (japan) SD 3104
1-3   lp: victor (japan) LS 105
december   cd: toshiba shinseido SGR 8114
1952

london   78: hmv DB 21618
9 may   45: hmv 7R 174
1953   45: hmv (italy) 7RQ 3036

schubert **piano trio no 1**

london	thibaud, violin	78: hmv DB 947-950
5-6	casals, cello	78: victor M 11
july		lp: hmv COLH 12
1926		lp: emi HLM 7017/1C047 01148M/

lp: emi HLM 7017/1C047 01148M/
RLS 723/1C153 52175-52177M/
3C161 50089-50091M

cd: emi CDH 761 0242/CDM 566 9862/
CHS 764 0572

cd: magic talent CD 48020

cd: monopoly GI 20059

cd: avid AMSC 586

cd: andante 1991-1994

cd: naxos 811.0188

third movement only

cd: emi CDZ 572 1542

ROBERT SCHUMANN (1810-1856)

piano concerto

hayes	albert hall	78: hmv DB 722-725
1 november	orchestra	78: victor 6516-6519
1923	ronald	lp: hmv COLH 31
		cd: biddulph LHW 021
		recording completed on 3 december 1923

london	london	78: hmv DB 1059-1062
22 june	symphony	78: victor M 46
1927	ronald	cd: music and arts CD 718
		cd: biddulph LHW 003

london	london	78: hmv DB 2181-2184
12 march	philharmonic	78: victor M 209
1934	ronald	lp: world records SHB 70
		cd: naxos 811.0612

berlin	rias-orchester	lp: replica RPL 2479
15 may	fricsay	cd: melodram CDM 18018
1951		

paris	conservatoire	hmv unpublished
2 january	orchestra	
1957	cluytens	

fantasiestücke

paris	hmv unpublished
27 december	
1956	

paris	hmv unpublished
5 february	
1957	

des abends/fantasiestücke

london	78: hmv DB 3338
26 october	78: victor M 573
1937	lp: angel GR 2128
	cd: pearl GEMMCD 9931
	cd: music and arts CD 4858
	cd: biddulph LHW 005

schumann **carnaval**

hayes 5 december 1923	78: hmv DB 706-708 cd: pearl GEMMCD 9932 cd: biddulph LHW 021
london 6 december 1927	hmv unpublished
london 5 june 1928	78: hmv DB 1252-1254 cd: music and arts CD 4858 cd: biddulph LHW 004 cd: philips 456 7512 *recording completed on 11 december 1928*
london 7-8 may 1953	lp: hmv ALP 1142 lp: hmv (italy) QALP 10065 lp: cmi 1C147 01544-01545M

davidsbündlertänze

london 18 may 1937	78: hmv DB 3263-3265 lp: cmi 1C147 01514-01515M cd: biddulph LHW 003

études symphoniques

london 11 march 1929	78: hmv DB 1325-1327 78: victor M 122 lp: angel GR 2031 cd: music and arts CD 4858 cd: pearl GEMMCD 9932 cd: biddulph LHW 004 cd: philips 456 7512
london 9 may 1953	lp: hmv ALP 1142 lp: hmv (italy) QALP 10065

schumann fantasy in c

london 6 july 1935	hmv unpublished
paris 26 december 1956	hmv unpublished

kinderszenen

london 4 july 1935	78: hmv DB 2581-2582 lp: emi 1C147 01544-01545M cd: pearl GEMMCD 9932 cd: biddulph LHW 005 cd: magic talent CD 48008 cd: philips 464 3812
london 9 october 1947	78: hmv DB 6700-6701 lp: victor LHMV 1009 cd: appian APR 5571
london 7-8 may 1953	hmv unpublished
paris 26 december 1956	hmv unpublished

der dichter spricht/kinderszenen

paris 1953	vhs video: warner/nvc 3984 291993 dvd video: warner/nvc 3984 291992 *recorded during a televised masterclass*

schumann **kreisleriana**

london 5 july 1935	78: hmv DB 2608-2611 78: victor M 493 lp: angel GR 2049/ GR 70017 lp: emi 1C147 01544-01545M cd: music and arts CD 858 cd: philips 456 7512 cd: biddulph LHW 005 cd: pearl GEMMCD 9931
london 28 june 1954	hmv unpublished
paris 26 december 1956	hmv unpublished
paris 5 february 1957	hmv unpublished

papillons

london 4 july 1935	78: hmv DA 1442-1443 78: victor 1819-1820 lp: emi HQM 1182/1C147 01544-01545M cd: pearl GEMMCD 9932 cd: biddulph LHW 003
london 27 october 1950	hmv unpublished
paris 27 december 1956	hmv unpublished
paris 5 february 1957	hmv unpublished

schumann vogel als prophet/waldszenen

london		78: hmv DA 1901
19 april		lp: hmv ALP 1197
1948		lp: hmv (italy) QALP 10080
		lp: emi HQM 1182

piano trio no 1

london   thibaud, violin   78: hmv DB 1209-1212
15-18   casals, cello   78: victor M 95
november   lp: emi HLM 7105/1C049 01808M/
1928   RLS 723/1C153 52475-52477M
cd: emi CHS 764 0572
cd: biddulph LHW 004
cd: monopoly GI 20059
cd: dutton CDBP 9726
recording completed on 3 december 1928

dichterliebe, song cycle

paris   panzéra, tenor   78: hmv DB 4987-4989
17-19   78: victor M 386
june   lp: angel GR 2162
1935   cd: pearl GEMMCD 9919
cd: dante HPC 004-005
cd: biddulph LHW 005
recording completed on 17 september 1935

paris   souzay, baritone   lp: hmv (france) FBLP 1090
17 july   lp: cetra LO 501
1957

ich grolle nicht/dichterliebe

paris   litvinne, soprano   g & t 33182
29 december   cd: symposium SYMCD 1101
1902   *subsequently re-recorded with another pianist*

ALEXANDER SCRIABIN (1872-1915)

étude pathétique/12 études op 8
camden nj	78: victor 982/66214
5 february	78: hmv DA 609
1923	cd: music and arts CD 615
	cd: biddulph LHW 014-015

may	duo-art piano roll 6623
1923	cd: nimbus NI 8814

IGOR STRAVINSKY (1882-1971)

danse russe/petrushka
london	hmv unpublished
6 december	
1927	

GIUSEPPE VERDI (1813-1901)

rigoletto paraphrase, arranged by liszt
camden nj	78: victor 6064/74636
28 january	78: hmv DB 168
1920	cd: biddulph LHW 014-015

camden nj	78: victor 6641/6681
27-28	78: hmv DB 1105
december	cd: pearl GEMMCD 9396/GEMMCD 9491
1926	cd: philips 456 7512

RICHARD WAGNER (1813-1883)

tristan und isolde, excerpt (mild und leise)

paris   litvinne, soprano   g & t 33162
29 december   *sung in french*   cd: symposium SYMCD 1101
1902   *subsequently re-recorded with another pianist*

die walküre, excerpt (hojotoho!)

paris   litvinne, soprano   g & t 33163
29 december   *sung in french*   cd: symposium SYMCD 1101
1902   *subsequently re-recorded with another pianist*

CARL MARIA VON WEBER (1786-1826)

piano sonata no 2

london   78: hmv DB 3799-3801
10 march   78: victor M 703
1939   lp: discocorp IGI 339
                             cd: music and arts CD 622/CD 4622
                             cd: biddulph LHW 002

aufforderung zum tanz

camden nj   78: victor 6064/74798
6 february   78: hmv DB 168
1923   cd: pearl GEMMCD 9386
                             cd: piano library PL 214
                             cd: biddulph LHW 014-015
                             this was an abridged version to fit one 78rpm side

camden nj   78: victor 1201
27-28   78: hmv DA 855
december   cd: pearl GEMMCD 9386
1926   cd: biddulph LHW 002

london   hmv unpublished
30 october
1950

alexis weissenberg

born 1929

JOHANN SEBASTIAN BACH (1685-1750)

goldberg variations

paris	lp: emi 1C151 11644-11645/
28 june-	2C165 11644-11645/2C167 11644-11645/
11 july	3C165 11645-11645
1967	lp: angel 3926
	cd: emi CZS 574 1442

paris	lp: emi 2C167 73091-73092
1-4	cd: emi CDE 575 0072/CDE 574 9532
june	
1981	

partita no 1

paris	lp: emi CVC 1914/2C167 11123-11125
12 april	cd: emi CZS 574 1442
1966	

partita no 2

paris	lp: emi CVC 1914/2C167 11123-11125
13 april	cd: emi CZS 574 1442
1966	

partita no 3

paris	lp: emi CVB 1897/2C167 11123-11125
15 april	cd: emi CZS 574 1442
1966	

partita no 4

paris	lp: emi CVB 1897/2C167 11123-11125
24 february	cd: emi CZS 574 1442
1966	cd: philips 456 9882

lugano	cd: eremitage ERM 102
1969	cd: aura AUR 1172

locarno	cd: eremitage ERM 165
31 august	cd: aura AUR 1722
1982	

bach **partita no 5**

paris   lp: emi CVB 1915/2C167 11123-11125
14 april   lp: angel 36437
1966   cd: emi CZS 574 1442

partita no 6

paris   lp: emi CVB 1915/2C167 11123-11125
24-25   lp: angel 36437
february   cd: emi CZS 574 1442
1966

chromatic fantasy and fugue in d minor

paris   lp: emi CVB 1915/2C167 11123-11125
26 april   lp: angel 36437
1966   cd: emi CZS 574 1442

overture in the french style in b minor

paris   lp: emi CVB 1915
27-30   cd: emi CZS 574 1442
september
1966

italian concerto

paris   cd: emi CZS 574 1442
27-28   *unpublished emi lp recording*
june
1967

4 duetti/klavierübung III

paris   lp: emi CVC 1914/2C167 11123-11125
23 september
1966

bach **chaconne in d minor from the second violin partita, arranged by busoni**

paris	lp: emi ASD 2971/1C061 12505/
11-15	2C069 12505
december	lp: angel 37088
1972	cd: emi 112 5052

recordings in these sessions completed in january, june and july 1973

ich ruf' zu dir herr jesu christ, chorale prelude arranged by busoni

paris	lp: emi ASD 2971/1C061 12505/
11-15	2C069 12505
december	lp: angel 37088
1972	cd: emi 112 5052

recordings in these sessions completed in january, june and july 1973

jesu bleibet meine freude, chorale from cantata 147 arranged by hess

paris	lp: emi ASD 2971/1C061 12505/
11-15	2C069 12505
december	lp: angel 37088
1972	cd: emi 112 5052

recordings in these sessions completed in january, june and july 1973

locarno	cd: eremitage ERM 165
31 august	cd: aura AUR 1722
1982	

nun freut euch liebe christen g'mein, chorale prelude arranged by busoni

paris	lp: emi ASD 2971/1C061 12505/
11-15	2C069 12505
december	lp: angel 37088
1972	cd: emi 112 5052

recordings in these sessions completed in january, june and july 1973

bach nun komm der heiden heiland, chorale prelude arranged by busoni

paris
11-15
december
1972

lp: emi ASD 2971/1C061 12505/
    2C069 12505
lp: angel 37088
cd: emi 112 5052
recordings in these sessions completed in january, june and july 1973

prelude in b minor, arranged by siloti

paris
11-15
december
1972

lp: emi ASD 2971/1C061 12505/
    2C069 12505
lp: angel 37088
cd: emi 112 5052
recordings in these sessions completed in january, june and july 1973

bach **prelude and fugue in a minor, arranged by liszt**

| paris | lp: lumen (france) LD 3400 |
| 1950 | |

paris	lp: emi ASD 2971/1C061 12505/
11-15	2C069 12505
december	lp: angel 37088
1972	cd: emi 112 5052
	recordings in these sessions completed in january, june and july 1973

sicilienne from the flute sonata in g minor, arranged by lustner

paris	lp: emi ASD 2971/1C061 12505/
11-15	2C069 12505
december	lp: angel 37088
1972	cd: emi 112 5052
	recordings in these sessions completed in january, june and july 1973

toccata and fugue in d minor, arranged by busoni

paris	lp: emi ASD 2971/1C061 12505/
11-15	2C069 12505
december	lp: angel 37088
1972	cd: emi 112 5052
	recordings in these sessions completed in january, june and july 1973

BELA BARTOK (1881-1945)

piano concerto no 2

philadelphia	philadelphia	lp: victor LSC 3159/LSB 4010
10-12	orchestra	cd: rca/bmg 09026 613962/
november	ormandy	74321 886902
1969		

LUDWIG VAN BEETHOVEN (1770-1827)

piano concerto no 1

berlin	berlin	lp: emi SLS 5112/1C157 53060-53063/
27-28	philharmonic	2C165 53060-53063
september	karajan	lp: angel 3854
1977		cd: emi CDM 566 0902/CDM 769 3342/
		CMS 566 1122/CZS 252 1722

piano concerto no 2

berlin	berlin	lp: emi SLS 5112/1C157 53060-53063/
27-28	philharmonic	2C165 53060-53063
september	karajan	lp: angel 3854
1977		cd: emi CDM 566 0902/CDM 769 3342/
		CMS 566 1122/CZS 252 1722

piano concerto no 3

berlin	berlin	lp: emi SLS 5112/1C157 53060-53063/
20 september	philharmonic	2C165 53060-53063
1976	karajan	lp: angel 3854
		cd: emi CDM 566 0912/CDM 769 3352/
		CMS 566 1122/CZS 252 1722
		recording completed on 27-28 september 1977

piano concerto no 4

salzburg	berlin	unpublished radio broadcast
4 april	philharmonic	
1971	karajan	

berlin	berlin	lp: emi SLS 5112/1C157 53060-53063/
4-6	philharmonic	2C165 53060-53063/1C065 03853/
september	karajan	2C069 03853
1974		lp: angel 3854
		cd: emi CDM 566 0912/CDM 769 3352/
		CMS 566 1122/CZS 252 1722

osaka	berlin	unpublished radio broadcast
10 november	philharmonic	*recording also includes rehearsal extracts*
1977	karajan	

unpublished video recording of this concerto made in bulgaria in the 1980s also exists

beethoven **piano concerto no 5 "emperor"**

berlin	berlin	lp: emi ASD 3043/SLS 5112/1C065 02535/
26-27	philharmonic	2C069 02535/3C065 02535/
may	karajan	1C157 53060-53063/2C165 53060-53063
1974		lp: angel 32045/3854/37062
		cd: emi CDM 566 0922/CDM 769 3362/
		CMS 566 1122/CZS 252 1722

vienna	vienna	unpublished radio broadcast
2 march	philharmonic	
1975	karajan	

salzburg	berlin	unpublished radio broadcast
11 april	philharmonic	
1976	karajan	

piano sonata no 8 "pathétique"

paris	lp: emi 2C069 16271
april	lp: angel 37660
1978	*recording completed in may and september 1978*

piano sonata no 14 "moonlight"

paris	lp: emi 2C069 16271
april	lp: angel 37660
1978	*recording completed in may and september 1978*

beethoven **piano sonata no 23 "appassionata"**

paris	lp: emi 2C069 16271
april	lp: angel 37660
1978	*recording completed in may and september 1978*

rondo in c op 51 no 1

paris	lp: emi SLS 5112/1C157 53060-53063/
20 may	2C165 53060-53063
1977	lp: angel 3854
	cd: emi CDM 769 3362

rondo a capriccio in g "rage over a lost penny"

paris	lp: emi SLS 5112/1C157 53060-53063/
20 may	2C165 53060-53063
1977	lp: angel 3854
	cd: emi CDM 769 3362

bagatelle in a minor "für elise"

paris	lp: emi SLS 5112/1C157 53060-53063/
18 april	2C165 53060-53063
1978	lp: angel 3854
	cd: emi CDM 769 3362

32 variations in c minor on an original theme woO 80

paris	lp: emi SLS 5112/1C157 53060-53063/
21-23	2C165 53060-53063
may	lp: angel 3854
1977	cd: emi CDM 769 3362

JOHANNES BRAHMS (1833-1897)

piano concerto no 1

london	london	lp: emi ASD 2992/1C063 02435/
november	symphony	2C069 12598/3C065 12598
1972	giulini	

philadelphia	philadelphia	lp: emi ASD 143 5211
2 february	orchestra	lp: angel 38008
1983	muti	cd: emi CDD 763 8992

unpublished video recording of this concerto made in bulgaria in the 1980s also exists

piano concerto no 2

turin	rai torino	lp: cetra LAR 9
5 february	orchestra	cd: cetra ARCD 2030
1960	maag	

rhapsody in g minor op 79 no 2

lugano	cd: eremitage ERM 102
1969	cd: aura AUR 1172

violin sonata no 1

paris	mutter, violin	lp: emi SLS 143 4433
september		cd: emi CDC 747 2992/CDE 574 7252
1982		

violin sonata no 2

paris	mutter, violin	lp: emi SLS 143 4433
september		cd: emi CDC 747 2992/CDE 574 7252
1982		

violin sonata no 3

paris	mutter, violin	lp: emi SLS 143 4433
september		cd: emi CDC 747 2992/CDE 574 7252
1982		

FREDERIC CHOPIN (1810-1849)

piano concerto no 1

paris	conservatoire	lp: emi 1C063 10445/2C069 10445/
september	orchestra	CVB 2081/2C059 10445/
1967	skrowaczewski	3C065 10445
		lp: angel 3723
		cd: emi CDE 575 0132/CZS 767 4122/
		CDE 574 9582/CDE 574 9592/
		CZS 573 3172

piano concerto no 2

brescia	orchestra	cd: arkadia CDMP 460
14 june	gasparo da salo	
1967	orizio	

paris	conservatoire	lp: emi 1C063 10446/2C069 10446/
september	orchestra	CVB 2082/2C059 73055/
1967	skrowaczewski	3C065 10446
		lp: angel 3723
		cd: emi CDE 575 0132/CZS 767 4122/
		CDE 574 9582/CDE 573 9592/
		CZS 573 3172

andante spianato and grande polonaise for piano and orchestra

paris	conservatoire	lp: emi ASD 2371/1C063 10781/
september	orchestra	CVB 2082/2C059 73055/
1967	skrowaczewski	3C065 10781
		lp: angel 3723
		cd: emi CDM 769 0362/CZS 767 4122/
		CZS 573 3172

fantasy on polish airs for piano and orchestra

brescia	orchestra	cd: arkadia CDMP 460
14 june	gasparo da salo	
1967	orizio	

paris	conservatoire	lp: emi ASD 2371/1C063 10781/
september	orchestra	CVB 2083/3C065 10781
1967	skrowaczewski	lp: angel 3723
		cd: emi CDM 769 0362/CZS 767 4122/
		CZS 573 3172

chopin **krakowiak for piano and orchestra**

brescia	orchestra	cd: arkadia CDMP 460
14 june	gasparo da salo	
1967	orizio	

paris	conservatoire	lp: emi ASD 2371/1C063 10781/
september	orchestra	CVB 2083/3C065 10781
1967	skrowaczewski	lp: angel 3723
		cd: emi CDM 769 0362/CZS 767 4122

variations on mozart's la ci darem la mano for piano and orchestra

brescia	orchestra	cd: arkadia CDMP 460
14 june	gasparo da salo	
1967	orizio	

paris	conservatoire	lp: emi ASD 2371/1C063 10781/
september	orchestra	CVB 2083/3C065 10781
1967	skrowaczewski	lp: angel 3723
		cd: emi CDM 769 0362/CZS 767 4122

étude op 25 no 7

lugano	cd: eremitage ERM 102
1968	cd: aura AUR 1172

paris	lp: emi 2C069 16236
6 february	
1979	

impromptu no 1

paris	lp: emi 2C069 16236
5 february	
1979	

chopin **piano sonata no 2 "funeral march"**

paris
16-18
september
1975

lp: emi 2C069 14079
recording completed in april and october 1976

piano sonata no 3

new york
14-17
august
1967

lp: victor LSC 2984/RB 6743/SB 6743

paris
16-18
september
1975

lp: emi 2C069 14079
recording completed in april and october 1976

3 mazurkas: op 17 no 4; op 50 no 3; op 56 no 3

paris
december
1971

cd: emi CZS 573 8302
unpublished emi lp recordings

nocturne op 9 no 1

paris
25-26
march
1968

lp: emi SLS 838/1C187 10382-10383/
          2C165 10382-10383/3C165 10382-10383
lp: angel 3747
cd: emi CZS 573 8302
recordings completed in january and february 1969

nocturne op 9 no 2

paris
25-26
march
1968

lp: emi SLS 838/1C187 10382-10383/
          2C165 10382-10383/3C165 10382-10383
lp: angel 3747
cd: emi CZS 573 8302
recordings completed in january and february 1969

nocturne op 9 no 3

lugano
1969

cd: eremitage ERM 102
cd: aura AUR 1172

paris
25-26
march
1968

lp: emi SLS 838/1C187 10382-10383/
          2C165 10382-10383/3C165 10382-10383
lp: angel 3747
cd: emi CZS 573 8302
recordings completed in january and february 1969

chopin **nocturne op 15 no 1**

paris	lp: emi SLS 838/1C187 10382-10383/
25-26	2C165 10382-10383/3C165 10382-10383
march	lp: angel 3747
1968	cd: emi CZS 573 8302

nocturne op 15 no 2

lugano	cd: eremitage ERM 102
1969	cd: aura AUR 1172

paris	lp: emi SLS 838/1C187 10382-10383/
25-26	2C165 10382-10383/3C165 10382-10383
march	lp: angel 3747
1968	cd: emi CZS 573 8302

nocturne op 15 no 3

paris	lp: emi SLS 838/1C187 10382-10383/
25-26	2C165 10382-10383/3C165 10382-10383
march	lp: angel 3747
1968	cd: emi CZS 573 8302

nocturne op 27 no 1

paris	lp: emi SLS 838/1C187 10382-10383/
25-26	2C165 10382-10383/3C165 10382-10383
march	lp: angel 3747
1968	cd: emi CZS 573 8302

nocturne op 27 no 2

lugano	cd: eremitage ERM 102
1969	cd: aura AUR 1172

paris	lp: emi SLS 838/1C187 10382-10383/
25-26	2C165 10382-10383/3C165 10392-10383
march	lp: angel 3747
1968	cd: emi CZS 573 8302

emi recordings of chopin nocturnes completed in january and february 1969

chopin **nocturne op 32 no 1**

paris	lp: emi SLS 838/1C187 10382-10383/
25-26	2C165 10382-10383/3C165 10382-10383
march	lp: angel 3747
1968	cd: emi CZS 573 8302

nocturne op 32 no 2

paris	lp: emi SLS 838/1C187 10382-10383/
25-26	2C165 10382-10383/3C165 10382-10383
march	lp: angel 3747
1968	cd: emi CZS 573 8302

nocturne op 37 no 1

paris	lp: emi SLS 838/1C187 10382-10383/
25-26	2C165 10382-10383/3C165 10382-10383
march	lp: angel 3747
1968	cd: emi CZS 573 8302

nocturne op 37 no 2

paris	lp: emi SLS 838/1C187 10382-10383/
25-26	2C165 10382-10383/3C165 10382-10383
march	lp: angel 3747
1968	cd: emi CZS 573 8302

nocturne op 48 no 1

paris	lp: emi SLS 838/1C187 10382-10383/
25-26	2C165 10382-10383/3C165 10382-10383/
march	1C063 45580
1968	lp: angel 3747
	cd: emi CZS 573 8302

lugano	cd: eremitage ERM 102
1969	cd: aura AUR 1172

nocturne op 48 no 2

paris	lp: emi SLS 838/1C187 10382-10383/
25-26	2C165 10382-10383/3C165 10382-10383
march	lp: angel 3747
1968	cd: emi CZS 573 8302

nocturne op 55 no 1

paris	lp: emi SLS 838/1C187 10382-10383/
25-26	2C165 10382-10383/3C165 10382-10383
march	lp: angel 3747
1968	cd: emi CZS 573 8302

emi recordings of the chopin nocturnes were completed in january and february 1969

chopin **nocturne op 55 no 2**

paris	lp: emi SLS 838/1C187 10382-10383/
25-26	2C165 10382-10383/3C165 10382-10383
march	lp: angel 3747
1968	cd: emi CZS 573 8302

nocturne op 62 no 1

paris	lp: emi SLS 838/1C187 10382-10383/
25-26	2C165 10382-10383/3C165 10382-10383
march	lp: angel 3747
1968	cd: philips 456 9882
	cd: emi CZS 573 8302

nocturne op 62 no 2

paris	lp: emi SLS 838/1C187 10382-10383/
25-26	2C165 10382-10383/3C165 10382-10383
march	lp: angel 3747
1968	cd: philips 456 9882
	cd: emi CZS 573 8302

nocturne op 72 no 1

paris	lp: emi SLS 838/1C187 10382-10383/
25-26	2C165 10382-10383/3C165 10382-10383
march	lp: angel 3747
1968	cd: emi CZS 573 8302

nocturne in c sharp minor op posth.

paris	lp: emi SLS 838/1C187 10382-10383/
25-26	2C165 10382-10383/3C165 10382-10383
march	lp: angel 3747
1968	cd: emi CZS 573 8302

| lugano | cd: eremitage ERM 102 |
| 1969 | cd: aura AUR 1172 |

emi recordings of the chopin nocturnes were completed in january and february 1969

chopin **nocturne in c minor op posth.**

paris	lp: emi SLS 838/1C187 10382-10383/
25-26	2C165 10382-10383/3C165 10382-10383
march	lp: angel 3747
1968	*recordings completed in january and february 1969*

scherzo no 1

new york	lp: victor LSC 2984/RB 6743/SB 6743
14-17	
august	
1967	

lugano	cd: eremitage ERM 102
1969	cd: aura AUR 1172

scherzo no 2

new york	lp: victor LSC 2984/RB 6743/SB 6743
14-17	
august	
1967	

valses, complete set

paris	lp: emi 2C069 73107
28-30	*nos. 3, 8, 9, 10 and 13 only*
december	cd: emi CZS 573 8302
1981	*recordings in these sessions completed in*
	january 1982 and february 1983

CARL CZERNY (1791-1857)

variations on la ricordanza

paris	lp: lumen (france) LD 3400
1950	cd: philips 456 9882

CLAUDE DEBUSSY (1862-1918)

children's corner (doctor gradus ad parnassum; jimbo's lullaby; serenade for a doll; the snow is dancing; the little shepherd; golliwog's cakewalk)

paris
march
1968

lp: victor LSC 3090
cd: rca/bmg 74321 242142

hamburg
january-
february
1985

lp: dg 415 5101
cd: dg 415 5102/445 5472

estampes (pagodes; la soirée dans grenade; jardins sous la pluie)

hamburg
january-
february
1985

lp: dg 415 5101
cd: dg 415 5102/445 5472
cd: philips 456 9882

suite bergamasque (prélude; menuet; clair de lune; passepied)

paris
march
1968

lp: victor LSC 3090
cd: rca/bmg VD 60909
clair de lune only
cd: rca/bmg 74321 242142

hamburg
january-
february
1985

lp: dg 415 5101
cd: dg 415 5102/445 5472
clair de lune only
cd: dg 459 1352

clair de lune/suite bergamasque

paris
5 february
1979

lp: emi 2C069 16326

debussy **pour les arpeges composés/études**

paris march 1968	lp: victor LSC 3090
paris 5 february 1979	lp: emi 2C069 16326
hamburg january- february 1985	lp: dg 415 5101 cd: dg 415 5102/445 5472

la fille aux cheveux de lin/préludes livre 1

paris march 1968	lp: victor LSC 3090 cd: rca/bmg 74321 242142
hamburg january- february 1985	lp: dg 415 5101 cd: dg 415 5102/445 5472

l'isle joyeuse

paris march 1968	lp: victor LSC 3090
hamburg january- february 1985	lp: dg 415 5101 cd: dg 415 5102/445 5472

la plus que lente

paris march 1968	lp: victor LSC 3090 cd: rca/bmg 74321 242142
paris 5 february 1979	lp: emi 2C069 16326
hamburg january- february 1985	lp: dg 415 5101 cd: dg 415 5102/445 5472

CESAR FRANCK (1822-1890)

variations symphoniques pour piano et orchestre

berlin	berlin	lp: emi ASD 2872/EG 29 08531/
21-27	philharmonic	1C065 02374/2C069 02374/
september	karajan	3C065 02374
1972		lp: angel 32009/34416/34751/36905
		cd: emi CDM 764 7472/CDM 769 0082/
		CDM 769 3802

violin sonata in a

paris	mutter, violin	lp: emi SLS 143 4433
september		
1982		

GEORGE GERSHWIN (1898-1937)

rhapsody in blue

berlin	berlin	unpublished radio broadcast
8 may	philharmonic	*recorded at the orchestra's centenary revue*
1982	ozawa	*concert*
berlin	berlin	lp: emi ASD 143 6591
8-12	philharmonic	lp: angel 38050
june	ozawa	cd: emi CDC 747 1522
1983		

variations on i got rhythm for piano and orchestra

berlin	berlin	lp: emi ASD 143 6591
8-12	philharmonic	lp: angel 38050
june	ozawa	cd: emi CDC 747 1522
1983		

catfish row, symphonic suite from porgy and bess for two pianos and orchestra

berlin	berlin	lp: emi ASD 143 6591
8-12	philharmonic	lp: angel 38050
june	ozawa	cd: emi CDC 747 1522
1983	e. donohoe, second piano	

FRANZ JOSEF HAYDN (1732-1809)

piano sonata in c minor hobXVI/20

hollywood   lp: victor LSC 3111
19-23
july
1968

paris   lp: emi 1C065 12850/2C069 12850/
1974   3C065 12850

piano sonata in d hobXVI/37

hollywood   lp: victor LSC 3111
19-23
july
1968

paris   lp: emi 1C065 12850/2C069 12850/
1974   3C065 12850

piano sonata in e flat hobXVI/52

paris   lp: lumen (france) LD 3400
1950

hollywood   lp: victor LSC 3111
19-23
july
1968

paris   lp: emi 1C065 12850/2C069 12850/
1974   3C065 12850

locarno   cd: eremitage ERM 165
30 august   cd: aura AUR 1722
1984

FRANZ LISZT (1811-1886)

piano sonata in b minor
paris
1950

lp: lumen (france) LD 3404

paris
3-4
april
1967

lp: emi CVC 2024/2C069 10090
lp: angel 36383
recording completed on 22-26 june 1967

3 petrarch sonnets/années de pelerinage
paris
7april
1967

lp: emi CVC 2024/2C069 10090
lp: angel 36383
recording completed on 24 april 1967

consolations nos 1 and 4
paris
1950

lp: lumen (france) LD 3404

funérailles/harmonies poétiques et réligieuses
paris
1950

lp: lumen (france) LD 3404

hungarian rhapsodies nos 3 and 11
paris
1950

lp: lumen (france) LD 3404

liebestraum no 3
paris
6 february
1979

lp: emi 2C069 16326

valse-impromptu
paris
6 february
1979

lp: emi 2C069 16326

XAVIER MONTSALVATGE (born 1912)

5 canciones negras (cuba dentro de un piano; chévere; punto de habanera; cancion de cuna para dormir a un negrito; canto negro)

paris	caballé, soprano	lp: emi 2C069 16380
27 april-		cd: emi CZS 567 6812
5 may		
1979		

WOLFGANG AMADEUS MOZART (1756-1791)

piano concerto no 9

vienna	vienna	lp: emi 1C065 16289/2C069 16289
23-25	symphony	
june	giulini	
1978		

piano concerto no 21

vienna	vienna	lp: emi 1C065 16289/2C069 16289
23-25	symphony	
june	giulini	
1978		

paris	berlin	unpublished video recording
24 june	philharmonic	*weissenberg performs first and third movements*
1978	karajan	*only: karajan is soloist for second movement in*
		this televised performance

MODEST MUSSORGSKY (1839-1881)

pictures from an exhibition

paris	lp: emi 1C063 12043/2C069 12043/
june	3C065 12043
1971	cd: emi CDM 769 3812/CDR 573 7522

SERGEI PROKOFIEV (1891-1953)

piano concerto no 3

turin	rai torino	cd: arkadia CDMP 405/34005
5 january	orchestra	
1962	celibidache	

paris	orchestre	lp: emi ASD 2701/1C063 11301/
27-28	de paris	2C069 11301/3C065 11301
may	ozawa	lp: angel 36785/83512
1970		

piano sonata no 3

new york	lp: columbia (usa) ML 2099
20 january	cd: philips 456 9882
1949	

suggestion diabolique/4 pieces op 4

new york	lp: columbia (usa) ML 2099
20 january	cd: philips 456 9882
1949	

SERGEI RACHMANINOV (1873-1943)

piano concerto no 2

berlin	berlin	lp: emi ASD 2872/1C065 02374/
21-27	philharmonic	2C069 02374/3C065 02374
september	karajan	lp: angel 32009/34416/36905
1972		cd: emi CDM 769 3802
berlin	berlin	vhs video: dg 072 1043
26 september	philharmonic	laserdisc: dg 072 1041
1973	karajan	*second movement only*
		vhs video: dg 072 1963
		laserdisc: dg 072 1961

piano concerto no 3

chicago	chicago	lp: victor LSC 3040/SB 6807/AGL1-3366
27-28	symphony	cd: rca/bmg 09026 613962
november	pretre	
1967		
boston	boston	lp: boston symphony orchestra
1972	symphony	
	ozawa	
paris	orchestre	lp: emi 1C065 03764/2C069 03764
14-15	national	lp: angel 37722
september	bernstein	
1979		
berlin	berlin	emi unpublished
23 june	philharmonic	*information supplied by michael gray*
1987	ozawa	

unpublished video recording of this concerto made in 1980s in bulgaria also exists

rachmaninov **piano sonata no 1**
hamburg   cd: dg 427 4992
may   cd: philips 456 9882
1987

piano sonata no 2
hamburg   cd: dg 427 4992
may
1987

prelude in c sharp minor
new york   columbia (usa) unpublished
6 may
1950

hollywood   lp: victor LSC 7069
15 july   lp: victor (germany) DX 26.35043
1968   cd: rca/bmg GD 60568

prelude op 23 no 1
hollywood   lp: victor LSC 7069
19 july   lp: victor (germany) DX 26.35043
1968   cd: rca/bmg GD 60568

prelude op 23 no 2
hollywood   lp: victor LSC 7069
17 july   lp: victor (germany) DX 26.35043
1968   cd: rca/bmg GD 60568

prelude op 23 no 3
hollywood   lp: victor LSC 7069
18 july   lp: victor (germany) DX 26.35043
1968   cd: rca/bmg GD 60568

rachmaninov **prelude op 23 no 4**

hollywood	lp: victor LSC 7069
14 july	lp: victor (germany) DX 26.35043
1969	cd: rca/bmg GD 60568

prelude op 23 no 5

hollywood	lp: victor LSC 7069
25 july	lp: victor (germany) DX 26.35043
1968	cd: rca/bmg GD 60568

prelude op 23 no 6

new york	columbia (usa) unpublished
6 may	
1950	

hollywood	lp: victor LSC 7069
15 july	lp: victor (germany) DX 26.35043
1968	cd: rca/bmg GD 60568

prelude op 23 no 7

hollywood	lp: victor LSC 7069
17 july	lp: victor (germany) DX 26.35043
1968	cd: rca/bmg GD 60568

prelude op 23 no 8

hollywood	lp: victor LSC 7069
19 july	lp: victor (germany) DX 26.35043
1968	cd: rca/bmg GD 60568

prelude op 23 no 9

hollywood	lp: victor LSC 7069
17 july	lp: victor (germany) DX 26.35043
1968	cd: rca/bmg GD 60568

rachmaninov **prelude op 23 no 10**

hollywood	lp: victor LSC 7069
16 july	lp: victor (germany) DX 26.35043
1968	cd: rca/bmg GD 60568

prelude op 32 no 1

hollywood	lp: victor LSC 7069
15 july	lp: victor (germany) DX 26.35043
1969	cd: rca/bmg GD 60568

prelude op 32 no 2

hollywood	lp: victor LSC 7069
16 july	lp: victor (germany) DX 26.35043
1969	cd: rca/bmg GD 60568

prelude op 32 no 3

hollywood	lp: victor LSC 7069
18 july	lp: victor (germany) DX 26.35043
1969	cd: rca/bmg GD 60568

prelude op 32 no 4

new york	lp: victor LSC 7069
19 november	lp: victor (germany) DX 26.35043
1969	cd: rca/bmg GD 60568

prelude op 32 no 5

hollywood	lp: victor LSC 7069
15 july	lp: victor (germany) DX 26.35043
1969	cd: rca/bmg GD 60568

prelude op 32 no 6

hollywood	lp: victor LSC 7069
16 july	lp: victor (germany) DX 26.35043
1969	cd: rca/bmg GD 60568

rachmaninov **prelude op 32 no 7**
new york
11 december
1968

lp: victor LSC 7069
lp: victor (germany) DX 26.35043
cd: rca/bmg GD 60568

prelude op 32 no 8
hollywood
16 july
1969

lp: victor LSC 7069
lp: victor (germany) DX 26.35043
cd: rca/bmg GD 60568

prelude op 32 no 9
hollywood
18 july
1969

lp: victor LSC 7069
lp: victor (germany) DX 26.35043
cd: rca/bmg GD 60568

prelude op 32 no 10
hollywood
15 july
1969

lp: victor LSC 7069
lp: victor (germany) DX 26.35043
cd: rca/bmg GD 60568
cd: philips 456 9882

prelude op 32 no 11
hollywood
15 july
1969

lp: victor LSC 7069
lp: victor (germany) DX 26.35043
cd: rca/bmg GD 60568

rachmaninov **prelude op 32 no 12**

new york	columbia (usa) unpublished
6 may	
1950	

hollywood	lp: victor LSC 7069
16 july	lp: victor (germany) DX 26.35043
1968	cd: rca/bmg GD 60568

prelude op 32 no 13

hollywood	lp: victor LSC 7069
14 july	lp: victor (germany) DX 26.35043
1969	cd: rca/bmg GD 60568

songs: the answer; o cease thy singing maiden fair; the lilacs; o do not grieve; the storm; to the children; christ is risen; by my window; in the silent night; vocalise; how fair is this spot; loneliness; arion; the morn of life; the harvest of sorrow; day to night comparing; spring waters

paris	gedda, tenor	lp: emi ASD 2928/2C065 10585
29 june		cd: emi CDM 763 7312
1967		*recordings in this session completed on 9-11 june 1969*

MAURICE RAVEL (1875-1937)

piano concerto in g

paris	orchestre	lp: emi ASD 2701/1C063 11301
9-10	de paris	2C069 11301/3C065 11301
october	ozawa	lp: angel 36785
1970		

le tombeau de couperin

paris	lp: emi 1C063 12043/2C069 12043/
june	3C065 12043/3C163 50116-50118
1971	

valses nobles et sentimentales

stockholm	lp: emi CVB 1902/2C065 34173/
1964	3C163 50116-50118

CAMILLE SAINT-SAENS (1835-1921)

le carnaval des animaux, fantasy for two pianos and orchestra

paris	conservatoire	lp: emi CVL 1920/ESD 7020/
13-15	orchestra	1C053 14176/2C069 10973/
june	pretre	3C065 10973
1966	ciccolini,	cd: emi CDE 574 5872/CDE 574 7532
	first piano	

DOMENICO SCARLATTI (1685-1757)

sonatas: in b minor K 87/L 33; in f K 107/L 474; in a minor K 109/L 238; in f minor K 184/L 189

munich	lp: dg 415 5111
march	cd: dg 415 5112
1985	cd: philips 456 9882

sonatas: in g minor K 8/L 488; in g K 13/L 486; in e K 20/L 375; in c K 132/L 457; in e flat K 193/L 142; in e minor K 233/L 467; in c sharp minor K 247/L 256; in g minor K 450/L 338; in f minor K 481/L 187; in e K 531/L 430; in b flat K 544/L 497

munich	lp: dg 415 5111
march	cd: dg 415 5112
1985	

FRANZ SCHUBERT (1797-1828)

seligkeit

paris	harwood,	unpublished video recording
1970	soprano	*other lieder may also have been recorded*

ROBERT SCHUMANN (1810-1856)

abegg variations
paris
25 june
1970

lp: emi 2C069 10547/3C065 10547

album für die jugend
paris
25-28
june
1973

lp: emi 1C065 12578/2C069 12578/
3C065 12578

arabeske in c
paris
20 june
1970

lp: emi 2C069 10547/2C069 16326/
3C065 10547

carnaval
paris
2-4
july
1967

lp: emi CVC 2025/2C065 10473
lp: angel 36552

davidsbündlertänze
paris
7-9
september
1977

lp: emi 2C069 16210

études symphoniques
paris
18-20
june
1969

lp: emi 2C069 10547/3C065 10547
recording completed on 29-30 may 1970

locarno
31 august
1982

cd: eremitage ERM 165
cd: aura AUR 1722

unpublished video recording of the work made in 1980s in bulgaria also exists

schumann **fantasy in c**
paris
12 may
1967

lp: emi CVB 2158/1C053 10091/
    2C069 10091
lp: angel 36616
recording completed on 16 october 1967

humoreske in b flat
paris
6 september
1977

lp: emi 2C069 16210

kinderszenen
paris
26 june
1968

lp: emi CVB 2158/1C053 10091/
    2C069 10091
lp: angel 36616
träumerei only
lp: emi 2C069 16326

piano sonata no 2
paris
2-4
july
1967

lp: emi CVC 2025/2C065 10473
lp: angel 36552

vogel als prophet/waldszenen
paris
9-12
september
1977

lp: emi 2C069 16210

ALEXANDER SCRIABIN (1872-1915)

étude op 8 no 11

new york   lp: columbia (usa) ML 2099
20 january   cd: philips 456 9882
1949

paris   lp: emi 2C069 16326
5 february
1979

nocturne in d flat for the left hand

new york   78: columbia (argentina) C 266566
20 january   lp: columbia (usa) ML 2099
1949   cd: philips 456 9882

paris   lp: emi 2C069 16326
5 february
1979

ANTONIO SOLER (1729-1783)

sonatas: no 1 in d minor; no 2 in c sharp minor; no 4 in d minor
paris   lp: lumen (france) LD 3400
1950

RICHARD STRAUSS (1864-1949)

lieder: wiegenlied; wie sollten wir geheim sie halten; die nacht; ich schwebe; heimliche aufforderung; waldseligkeit; als mir dein lied erklang; zueignung; schlechtes wetter; ruhe meine seele; freundliche vision; des dichters abendgang; ich trage meine minne; traum durch die dämmerung; ständchen
paris   caballé, soprano   lp: emi 2C069 16381
27 april-
5 may
1979

IGOR STRAVINSKY (1882-1971)

three movements from petrushka (danse russe; chez pétrouchka; la semaine grasse)
stockholm   lp: emi CVC 1902/2C065 34173/
1964   3C163 50116-5011888
                                   cd: philips 456 9882
                                   also unpublished video recording: film
                                   version produced by ingmar bergman

PIOTR TCHAIKOVSKY (1840-1893)

piano concerto no 1

berlin	berlin	vhs video: dg 072 1413
april	philharmonic	laserdisc: dg 072 1411
1967	karajan	

paris	orchestre	lp: emi ASD 2576/1C065 02044/
february	de paris	2C069 02044/3C065 02044
1970	karajan	lp: angel 32042/36755
		cd: emi CDM 769 3812

berlin	berlin	laserdisc: japan 072 1041/072 2041/
september	philharmonic	VHM 68052
1973	karajan	

salzburg	berlin	unpublished radio broadcast
5 june	philharmonic	
1976	karajan	

berceuse/18 morceaux op 72

paris	lp: emi 2C069 16326
april	
1978	

JOAQUIN TURINA (1882-1949)

canto a sevilla (preludio; semana santa; las fuentecitos del parque; noche de feria; el fantasma; la gualda; ofrenda

paris	caballé, soprano	lp: emi 2C069 16380
27 april-		cd: emi CZS 567 6812
5 may		
1979		

MISCELLANEOUS

in a recent tv documentary weissenberg recalls 1967 recordings of jazz selections, some made in conjunction with the singer charles trenet

sir clifford curzon

1907-1982

CEP 524

FRANCK

Variations Symphoniques

FOR PIANO AND ORCHESTRA

Clifford CURZON with

The LONDON PHILHARMONIC ORCHESTRA conducted by

SIR ADRIAN BOULT

LUDWIG VAN BEETHOVEN (1770-1827)

piano concerto no 4

vienna 1-5 april 1954	vienna philharmonic knappertsbusch	lp: decca LXT 2948/ECM 572/ECS 572 lp: london (usa) LLP 1045/CM 9108 cd: decca 467 1262
munich 14-15 february 1977	bavarian radio orchestra kubelik	cd: audite 95.459

piano concerto no 5 "emperor"

london 12-13 september 1949	london philharmonic szell	78: decca AX 282-286 78: decca (switzerland) AK 2281-2285 78: london (usa) LA 123 lp: decca LXT 2506 lp: decca (germany) 648.112 lp: london (usa) LLP 114/LLC 17504
vienna 10-15 june 1957	vienna philharmonic knappertsbusch	lp: decca LXT 5391/SXL 2002/SPA 334 lp: london (usa) LLP 1757/CM 9217/ CS 6019/JL 41020 cd: decca 421 6162/452 3022/467 1262 *also issued on lp in a private edition by preiser*
london 17 february 1971	bbc symphony boulez	cd: bbc legends BBCL 40202
munich 14-15 february 1977	bavarian radio orchestra kubelik	cd: audite 95.459
london 4 september 1980	scottish national orchestra gibson	unpublished radio broadcast

beethoven **eroica variations and fugue**

london	lp: decca SXL 6523
17-21	lp: london (usa) CS 6727
december	cd: decca 452 3022
1970	*recording completed on 14-17 april 1971*

rondo a capriccioso in g "rage over a lost penny"

london	decca unpublished
29 october	
1942	

LILI BOULANGER (1893-1918)

3 pieces pour violon et piano

london	menuhin, violin	lp: emi ASD 2392
27 december		cd: emi CDM 764 2812
1967		

JOHANNES BRAHMS (1833-1897)

piano concerto no 1

walthamstow 5 june 1946	national symphony orchestra jorda	78: decca K 1491-1496 cd: dutton CDEA 5507 cd: pearl GEM 0041
new york 4 february 1951	new york philharmonic walter	unpublished radio broadcast
amsterdam may 1953	concertgebouw orchestra beinum	lp: decca LXT 2825/ACL 227 lp: london (usa) LLP 850 cd: decca 421 1432
london 30 may- 1 june 1962	london symphony szell	lp: decca LXT 6023/SXL 6023 lp: london (usa) CM 9329/CS 6329 cd: decca 417 6412/425 0822/466 3762

piano concerto no 2

salzburg 26 july 1955	vienna philharmonic knappertsbusch	cd: melodram GM 40039
vienna 21-24 october 1957	vienna philharmonic knappertsbusch	lp: decca LXT 5434/ECM 571/ ECS 571/ACL 320 cd: decca 460 9942

brahms **piano sonata no 3**

london

june

1962

lp: decca LXT 6041/SXL 6041

lp: london (usa) CM 9341/CS 6341/
STS 15272

cd: decca 448 5782

piano quartet no 2

new york	members of	lp: columbia (usa) ML 4630/
27-28	budapest	3226 0019
april	string quartet	lp: philips ABL 3122/A01192L
1952		

piano quintet in f minor

new york	budapest	lp: columbia (usa) ML 4336/
2-3	string quartet	3216 0173
may		
1950		

london	amadeus	cd: bbc legends BBCL 40092
17 november	string quartet	
1974		

liebeslieder-walzer, for vocal quartet and 2 pianos

edinburgh	seefried,soprano	lp: decca 417 6341
2 september	ferrier,contralto	cd: decca 425 9952
1952	patzak, tenor	
	günter, baritone	
	gal, second piano	

zum schluss/neue liebeslieder-walzer for vocal quartet and 2 pianos

edinburgh	seefried,soprano	lp: decca 417 6341
2 september	ferrier,contralto	cd: decca 425 9952
1952	patzak, tenor	
	günter, baritone	
	gal, second piano	

brahms capriccio op 76 no 2
london · decca unpublished
26 november
1943

intermezzo op 117 no 1
london · decca unpublished
26 november
1943

london · lp: decca LXT 6041/SXL 6041
june · lp: london (usa) CM 9341/CS 6341/
1962 ·   STS 15272
· cd: decca 417 6412/448 5782

london · unpublished radio broadcast
17 november
1974

intermezzo op 118 no 6
london · decca unpublished
26 november
1943

london · unpublished radio broadcast
17 november
1974

intermezzo op 119 no 3
london · decca unpublished
26 november
1943

london · lp: decca LXT 6041/SXL 6041
june · lp: london (usa) CM 9341/CS 6341/
1962 ·   STS 15272
· cd: decca 417 6412/448 5782

rhapsody op 79 no 2
london · decca unpublished
26 november
1943

BENJAMIN BRITTEN (1913-1976)

introduction and rondo alla burlesca for 2 pianos

london	britten,	78: decca K 1117
5 january	first piano	cd: pearl GEMMCD 9177
1944		

mazurka elegiaca for 2 pianos

london	britten,	78: decca K 1118
5 january	first piano	cd: pearl GEMMCD 9177
1944		

FREDERIC CHOPIN (1810-1849)

nocturne in c sharp minor op posth.

london	decca unpublished
21 july	
1949	

london	decca unpublished
15 october	
1951	

ANTONIN DVORAK (1841-1904)

piano quintet op 81

new york	budapest	lp: columbia (usa) ML 4825/3226 0019
18-19	string quartet	
april		
1953		

vienna	vienna	lp: decca LXT 6043/SXL 6043/SDD 270
october	philharmonic	lp: london (usa) CM 9357/CS 6357
1962	quartet	cd: decca 421 1532/448 6022

MANUEL DE FALLA (1876-1946)

noches en los jardinos de espana

london	national	78: decca K 1158-1160
26 september	symphony	cd: dutton CDK 1202
1945	orchestra	cd: pearl GEM 0041
	jorda	*recording completed on 17 march 1947*

london	new symphony	lp: decca LXT 2621/LXT 5165/ACL 102
2 july	orchestra	lp: london (usa) LLP 1397
1951	jorda	

CESAR FRANCK (1822-1890)

variations symphoniques pour piano et orchestre

london	london	45: decca CEP 524
14-15	philharmonic	lp: decca LXT 5547/SXL 2173/JB 104
december	boult	lp: london (usa) CM 9029/CS 6157/
1955		STS 15407
		cd: decca 425 0822/433 6282/466 3762

piano quintet in f minor

new york	budapest	lp: columbia (usa) Y 33315
18 december	string quartet	
1956		

vienna	vienna	lp: decca LXT 5640/SXL 2278/SDD 277
16 october	philharmonic	lp: london (usa) CM 9294/CS 6226
1960	quartet	cd: decca 421 1532

EDVARD GRIEG (1843-1907)

piano concerto

london	london	lp: decca LXT 2657/LXT 5165/ACL 102/
15 october	symphony	ECM 514/ECS 514/ECS 753
1951	fistoulari	lp: london (usa) LLP 1397
london	london	lp: decca LXT 5547/SXL 2173
22-23	symphony	lp: london (usa) CM 9029/CS 6157
june	fjeldstad	cd: decca 433 6282/448 5992/460 9942
1959		

FRANZ JOSEF HAYDN (1732-1809)

andante and variations in f minor

london	cd: bbc legends BBCL 40782
30 march	
1961	

FRANZ LISZT (1811-1886)

piano sonata in b minor

edinburgh
5 september
1961

cd: bbc legends BBCL 40782

london
april
1963

lp: decca LXT 6076/SXL 6076
lp: london (usa) CM 9371/CS 6371
cd: decca 452 3062

sonetto 104 del petrarca/années de pelerinage

london
29 october
1942

78: decca M 527

edinburgh
5 september
1961

cd: bbc legends BBCL 40782

liebestraum no 3

london
9 september
1947

78: decca K 1724

london
april
1963

lp: decca LXT 6076/SXL 6076
lp: london (usa) CM 9371/CS 6371
cd: decca 452 3062

liszt **mephisto waltz no 1**
london   decca unpublished
29 october
1942

london   78: decca K 1723-1724
9 september   cd: pearl GEM 0027
1947   cd: history 20.3175.306

gnomenreigen/études de concert
london   lp: decca LXT 6076/SXL 6076
april   lp: london (usa) CM 9371/CS 6371
1963   cd: decca 452 3062

berceuse
edinburgh   cd: bbc legends BBCL 40782
5 september
1961

london   lp: decca LXT 6076/SXL 6076
april   lp: london (usa) CM 9371/CS 6371
1963   cd: decca 452 3062

valse oubliée no 1
edinburgh   cd: bbc legends BBCL 40782
5 september
1961

london   lp: decca LXT 6076/SXL 6076
april   lp: london (usa) CM 9371/CS 6371
1963   cd: decca 452 3062

HENRY LITOLFF (1818-1891)

scherzo/concerto symphonique no 4

london	london	decca unpublished
14-15	philharmonic	
december	boult	
1955		

london	london	lp: decca LXT 5547/SXL 2173/
14-15	philharmonic	JB 29/JB 104
december	boult	lp: london (usa) CM 9029/CS 6157/
1958		STS 15407
		cd: decca 425 0822/466 3762

NIKOLAI MEDTNER (1880-1951)

skazka in f minor/4 fairy tales

london	decca unpublished
29 october	
1942	

WOLFGANG AMADEUS MOZART (1756-1791)

piano concerto no 20

snape	english chamber	lp: decca SXL 7007
24 september	orchestra	lp: london (usa) CS 7251
1970	britten	cd: decca 417 2882/468 4912

piano concerto no 21

munich	bavarian radio	cd: madrigal (japan) MADR 215
16 december	orchestra	cd: audite 95.453
1976	kubelik	

piano concerto no 23

london	national	78: decca K 1394-1396
12 december	symphony	cd: history 20.3175.306
1945	orchestra	cd: dutton CDEA 5507
	neel	cd: pearl GEM 0027

london	london	lp: decca LXT 2867
12-14	symphony	lp: decca (france) 411 6781
october	krips	lp: london (usa) LLP 918
1953		

vienna	vienna	decca unpublished
7-10	philharmonic	
december	szell	
1964		

london	london	lp: decca LXT 6354/SXL 6354
1-4	symphony	lp: london (usa) CS 6580
december	kertesz	cd: decca 452 8882/468 4912
1967		*468 4912 gives recording date as october 1967*

würzburg	bavarian radio	cd: madrigal (japan) MADR 215
21 june	orchestra	cd: audite 95.466
1975	kubelik	

mozart **piano concerto no 24**

london	london	lp: decca LXT 2867
12-14	symphony	lp: decca (france) 411 6781
october	krips	lp: london (usa) LLP 918
1953		

london	london	lp: decca LXT 6354/SXL 6354
6-11	symphony	lp: london (usa) CS 6580
october	kertesz	cd: decca 452 8882/468 4912
1967		*468 4912 gives recording date as december 1967*

munich	bavarian radio	cd: audite 95.453
17 january	orchestra	
1970	kubelik	

salzburg	vienna	unpublished radio broadcast
27 july	philharmonic	
1975	abbado	

piano concerto no 26 "coronation"

london	london	cd: decca 468 4912
1-4	symphony	cd: philips 456 7572
december	kertesz	*unpublished decca lp recording, which was*
1967		*allocated catalogue number SXL 6492*

london	bbc symphony	cd: bbc legends BBCL 40202
14 august	orchestra	
1974	boulez	

mozart **piano concerto no 27**

vienna 7-10 december 1964	vienna philharmonic szell	decca unpublished
london 6-11 october 1967	london symphony kertesz	cd: philips 456 7572 *unpublished decca lp recording, which was allocated catalogue number SXL 6492*
munich 15 january 1970	bavarian radio orchestra kubelik	cd: audite 95.466
snape 25 september 1970	english chamber orchestra britten	lp: decca SXL 7007 lp: london (usa) CS 7251 cd: decca 417 2882/468 4912
amsterdam 22 december 1972	concertgebouw orchestra haitink	cd: q-disc 97014
london 11 september 1979	english chamber orchestra barenboim	cd: bbc legends BBCL 40372

concerto for 2 pianos

london 11 september 1979	english chamber orchestra barenboim, second piano and conductor	cd: bbc legends BBCL 40372

mozart **piano quartet no 1**

london	members of	lp: decca LXT 2772/ECM 523/ECS 523
9-11	amadeus	lp: london (usa) CM 9061
september	string quartet	cd: decca 425 9602
1952		

piano quartet no 2

washington dc	members of	cd: music and arts CD 643
april	budapest	
1951	string quartet	

london	members of	lp: decca LXT 2772/ECM 523/ECS 523
9-11	amadeus	lp: london (usa) CM 9061
september	string quartet	cd: decca 425 9602
1952		

WILLEM PIJPER (1894-1947)

symphony no 3 with piano obbligato

amsterdam	concertgebouw	lp: decca LXT 2873
may	orchestra	
1953	van beinum	

SERGEI RACHMANINOV (1873-1943)

piano concerto no 2

london	london	lp: decca LXT 5119/LXT 5178/LW 5296/
27-28	philharmonic	ACL 159/ACL 322/ECS 753
june	boult	lp: london (usa) LLP 1294/LLP 1424/
1955		CM 9142
		cd: decca 460 9942

ALAN RAWSTHORNE (1905-1971)

piano concerto no 2

london	london	lp: decca LX 3066
29-30	symphony	lp: london (usa) LS 513
october	sargent	
1951		

FRANZ SCHUBERT (1797-1828)

wanderer fantasy, version for piano and orchestra arranged by liszt

london	queen's hall	78: decca X 185-187
1 april	orchestra	cd: history 20.3175.306
1937	wood	cd: pearl GEM 0027

wanderer fantasy, version for piano solo

london	decca unpublished
10 september	
1947	

london	lp: decca LX 3059
19 july	lp: london (usa) LPS 83
1949	cd: philips 456 7572
	cd: decca 466 4982

piano sonata no 17 d850

london	lp: decca LXT 6135/SXL 6135
11-15	lp: london (usa) CM 9416/CS 6416
june	cd: decca 443 5702
1964	

piano sonata no 21 d960

london	lp: decca SXL 6580
15-17	lp: london (usa) CS 6801
september	cd: decca 448 5782/452 3992
1972	*recording completed on 17-19 november 1972*

salzburg	cd: orfeo C401951B
26 august	
1974	

schubert **6 moments musicaux**

london
5 6
february
1971

lp: decca SXL 6523
lp: london (usa) CS 6727
cd: decca 443 5702

impromptu d899 no 1

london
4 june
1941

78: decca K 1018
cd: pearl GEM 0027
cd: history 20.3175.306
cd: philips 456 7572
recording completed in november and december 1941

impromptu d899 no 2

london
4 june
1941

78: decca K 1019
cd: philips 456 7572
recording completed on 11 november 1941

london
24 december
1961

cd: bbc legends BBCL 40782

impromptu d899 no 3

london
4 june
1941

78: decca K 1019
cd: philips 456 7572

london
24 december
1961

cd: bbc legends BBCL 40782

london
11-15
june
1964

lp: decca LXT 6135/SXL 6135
lp: london (usa) CM 9416/CS 6416
cd: decca 443 5702

schubert **impromptu d899 no 4**

london
4 june
1941

78: decca K 1020
cd: philips 456 7572

london
24 december
1961

cd: bbc legends BBCL 40782

london
11-15
june
1964

lp: decca LXT 6135/SXL 6135
lp: london (usa) CM 9416/CS 6416
cd: decca 443 5702

impromptu d935 no 1

london
9-11
december
1952

lp: decca LXT 2781/LW 5135
lp: london (usa) LLP 720
cd: philips 456 7572

schubert **impromptu d935 no 2**

london	decca unpublished
21 july	
1949	

london	lp: decca LXT 2781/LW 5135
9-11	lp: london (usa) LLP 720
december	cd: philips 456 7572
1952	

london	lp: decca SXL 6580
4-5	lp: london (usa) CS 6801
february	cd: decca 452 3062
1971	

impromptu d935 no 3

london	lp: decca LXT 2781/LW 5108
9-11	lp: london (usa) LLP 720
december	cd: philips 456 7572
1952	

impromptu d935 no 4

london	lp: decca LXT 2781/LW 5108
9-11	lp: london (usa) LLP 720
december	cd: philips 456 7572
1952	

schubert **piano quintet in a "trout"**

vienna october 1957	members of vienna octet	lp: decca LXT 5433/SXL 2110/ ADD 185/SDD 185 lp: london (usa) CM 9234/CS 6090 cd: decca 448 6022
london 1 february 1971	amadeus string quartet	cd: bbc legends BBCL 40092
snape september- october 1977	amadeus string quartet	lp: cbs 79316

ROBERT SCHUMANN (1810-1856)

piano sonata no 2
london   decca unpublished
11 november
1941

fantasy in c
london   lp: decca LXT 2933
1-3   lp: london (usa) LLP 1009
march   cd: decca 466 4982
1954

salzburg   cd: orfeo C401 951B
26 august
1974

kinderszenen
london   lp: decca LXT 2933
1-3   lp: london (usa) LLP 1009
march   cd: decca 466 4982
1954

piano quintet op 44
washington dc   budapest   cd: music and arts CD 643
april   string quartet
1951

new york   budapest   lp: columbia 33CX 1050
28-29   string quartet   lp: columbia (usa) ML 4426/3226 0019
april
1951

adagio and allegro in a flat for cello and piano
prades   casals, cello   cd: as-disc AS 350
july
1956

PIOTR TCHAIKOVSKY (1840-1893)

piano concerto no 1

london 13 december 1944	national symphony orchestra sargent	decca unpublished
london 5-9 september 1950	new symphony orchestra szell	78: decca X 53059-53062 lp: decca LXT 2559 lp: decca (germany) 648.112 lp: london (usa) LLP 276/LLC 17505

vienna 14-17 october 1958	vienna philharmonic solti	lp: decca BR 3042/SXL 2114/
		    ADD 191/SDD 191
		lp: london (usa) CM 9045/CS 6100/
		    STS 15471
		cd: decca 417 6762/421 6762/
		    436 5322/460 9942

solomon cutner

1902-1988

drawing by brian pinder

JOHANN SEBASTIAN BACH (1685-1750)

italian concerto
berlin   cd: appian APR 7030
23 february
1956

wachet auf, chorale prelude arranged by busoni
london   78: hmv C 3768
20 may   78: hmv (norway) ZN 556
1948   *also issued by hmv in the netherlands*

prelude and fugue in a minor, arranged by liszt
london   78: hmv C 3376
2 december   78: hmv (australia) EB 309
1943   lp: emi 1C147 53382-53389
                                              cd: philips 456 9732

prelude and fugue in g bwv 860/wohltemperiertes klavier I
london   cd: testament SBT 1042
21 august   *unpublished hmv lp recording*
1952

prelude and fugue in c minor bwv 871/wohltemperiertes klavier II
london   45: hmv 7P 123
15 september   lp: emi 1C147 53382-53389
1951

LUDWIG VAN BEETHOVEN (1170-1827)

piano concerto no 1

london	philharmonia	lp: hmv ALP 1583/ASD 294
16-17	menges	lp: emi SLS 5026/1C147 01671-01673
september		lp: angel 35580/60016
1956		cd: emi CZS 767 7352/CDF 300 0041
		cd: testament SBT 1219
		recording completed on 26 september 1956

piano concerto no 2

london	philharmonia	lp: hmv BLP 1024
3-6	cluytens	lp: hmv (france) FBLP 1055
november		lp: hmv (italy) QBLP 5012
1952		lp: electrola E 70027/WBLP 1024
		lp: victor LHMV 12
		lp: emi SLS 5026/1C147 01671-01673/ MFP 2067
		lp: angel 60308
		cd: emi CDF 300 0042/CHS 565 5032
		cd: testament SBT 1219
		LHMV 12 incorrectly named conductor as ackermann

berlin	berlin	cd: myto MCD 89005
27 february	philharmonic	
1956	cluytens	

beethoven piano concerto no 3

bedford	bbc symphony	78: hmv DB 6196-6199/8973-8976 auto
8-11	boult	78: hmv (australia) ED 409-412/
august		ED 1156-1159 auto
1944		45: victor WHMV 1035
		lp: victor LHMV 12/LHMV 1035
		cd: emi CHS 565 5032

*according to michael gray these victor editions of
the performance were not published*

amsterdam	concertgebouw	cd: q-disc 97015
18 december	orchestra	
1952	beinum	

london	philharmonia	lp: hmv ALP 1546/BSD 751
17-19	menges	lp: hmv (spain) SREG 1503
september		lp: angel 60019
1956		lp: world records T 540/ST 540
		lp: emi SLS 5026/1C147 01671-01673
		cd: emi CZS 767 7352/CDF 300 0042
		cd: testament SBT 1220

*according to bryan crimp an incomplete radio broadcast of the concerto with solomon and
the san francisco symphony orchestra conducted by monteux may also survive*

piano concerto no 4

london	philharmonia	lp: hmv BLP 1036
3-5	cluytens	lp: hmv (france) FBLP 1056
november		lp: hmv (italy) QBLP 5016
1952		lp: electrola E 70032/WBLP 1036
		lp: victor LHMV 1056
		lp: emi SLS 5026/XLP 30020/
		1C147 01671-01673
		cd: emi CDF 300 0042/CHS 565 5032
		cd: testament SBT 1220

beethoven **piano concerto no 5 "emperor"**

london	philharmonia	lp: hmv ALP 1300
13-15	menges	lp: victor LM 2108
may		lp: angel AHA 17/60298
1955		lp: emi SLS 5026/1C147 01671-01673/
		1C147 53382-53389
		cd: emi CDF 300 0042/CHS 565 5032
		cd: testament SBT 1221

piano sonata no 1

london	lp: hmv ALP 1573
22 june	lp: electrola E 90900/33WCX 1575
1952	lp: victor LM 1821
	lp: emi RLS 722/1C147 52448-52454M
	cd: testament SBT 1188

piano sonata no 3

london	78: hmv C 3847-3849/C 7747-7749 auto
21 may	78: hmv (norway) ZN 561-563
1948	lp: victor LM 1821
	lp: emi RLS 722/1C147 52448-52454M
	cd: pearl GEM 0038

london	cd: testament SBT 1188
25 may	*unpublished hmv lp recording*
1951	

berlin	cd: appian APR 7030
23 february	
1956	

beethoven **piano sonata no 7**
london
22 23
august
1956

lp: hmv ALP 1573
lp: electrola E 90900/33WCX 1573
lp: emi RLS 722/1C147 52448-52454M
cd: testament SBT 1189

piano sonata no 8 "pathétique"
london
22 june
1951

78: hmv C 4117-4119/C 7871-7873 auto
45: victor WDM 1654
lp: hmv ALP 1062
lp: hmv (spain) REG 1064
lp: victor LM 1222
lp: angel 60286
lp: emi 1C047 01478M
cd: emi CDF 300 0042
cd: testament SBT 1189
also issued on 78rpm by hmv in netherlands

piano sonata no 13
london
9 january
1956

lp: hmv ALP 1900
lp: emi RLS 722/1C147 52448-52454M
cd: testament SBT 1189

piano sonata no 14 "moonlight"
london
21 june
1945

78: hmv C 3455-3456
78: hmv (australia) EB 261-262
cd: emi CHS 565 5032
*recording completed in july and august 1945;
also issued on 78rpm in netherlands and india*

london
21 august
1952

lp: hmv BLP 1051
lp: hmv (spain) REG 1964
lp: electrola E 70037/WBLP 1051
lp: angel 60286
lp: emi RLS 722/1C147 52448-52454M/
    1C047 01478M
cd: testament SBT 1189

berlin
23 february
1956

cd: appian APR 7030

beethoven **piano sonata no 17 "tempest"**

london	lp: hmv ALP 1303
21 december	lp: victor LM 1964
1954	lp: emi RLS 722/1C147 52448-52454M
	cd: testament SBT 1190

piano sonata no 18

london	lp: hmv ALP 1303
5 november	lp: emi RLS 701/1E 01378-01380M/
1954	RLS 722/1C147 52448-52454M
	cd: testament SBT 1190

piano sonata no 21 "waldstein"

london	45: victor WDM 1716
15 june	lp: hmv ALP 1160
1952	lp: hmv (italy) QALP 10170
	lp: victor LM 1716
	lp: emi HQM 1077/RLS 722/
	1C147 52448-52454M/
	1C147 53382-53389
	lp: turnabout THS 65068-65070
	cd: testament SBT 1190

beethoven **piano sonata no 22**
london
16 may
1951

78: hmv C 4159
78: hmv (australia) EB 565
45: victor WDM 1716
lp: hmv ALP 1546
lp: victor LM 1716
lp: world records T 540/ST 540
lp: emi RLS 722/1C147 52448-52454M
cd: testament SBT 1190

piano sonata no 23 "appassionata"
london
24 october
1954

lp: hmv ALP 1272
lp: hmv (italy) QALP 10176
lp: victor LM 1964
lp: angel AHA 11
lp: emi RLS 722/1C147 52448-52454M
cd: testament SBT 1192

piano sonata no 26 "les adieux"
london
20-21
november
1952

45: victor WDM 1733
lp: hmv BLP 1051
lp: hmv (spain) REG 1064
lp: electrola E 70037/WBLP 1051
lp: angel 60308
lp: emi RLS 722/1C147 52448-52454M/
    1C047 01478M
cd: testament SBT 1191

piano sonata no 27
london
21-22
august
1956

lp: hmv ALP 1583/ASD 294
lp: angel 35580/60016
lp: emi XLP 30020/RLS 722/
    1C147 52448-52454M
cd: emi CHS 764 7082/CZS 767 7352
cd: testament SBT 1191

beethoven **piano sonata no 28**

london	lp: hmv ALP 1272
20 december	lp: hmv (italy) QALP 10176
1954	lp: angel AHA 11
·	lp: emi XLP 30116/1C047 01936M/
	RLS 722/1C147 52448-52454M
	lp: turnabout THS 65078-65080
	cd: emi CHS 764 7082
	cd: testament SBT 1192

piano sonata no 29 "hammerklavier"

london	45: victor WDM 1733
15-16	lp: hmv ALP 1141
september	lp: victor LM 1733
1952	lp: angel AHA 36
	lp: emi XLP 30116/1C047 01936M/
	RLS 722/1C147 52448-52454M
	lp: turnabout THS 65068-65070
	cd: emi CHS 764 7082
	cd: philips 456 9732
	cd: testament SBT 1191

piano sonata no 30

london	45: victor WDM 1716
19 june	lp: hmv ALP 1062
1951	lp: victor LM 1716
	lp: emi RLS 722/1C147 52448-52454M
	lp: turnabout THS 65068-65070
	cd: emi CHS 764 7082
	cd: testament SBT 1192

beethoven **piano sonata no 31**

london
20-21
august
1956

lp: hmv ALP 1900
lp: emi RLS 722/1C147 52448-52454M/
    1C047 01553
cd: emi CHS 764 7082
cd: testament SBT 1192

piano sonata no 32

london
21 may
1948

78: hmv C 4000-4003/C 7786-7789 auto
cd: testament SBT 1230
cd: pearl GEM 0038
*side one of this 78rpm recording was re-made
on 7 october 1948*

london
24 may
1951

45: victor WDM 1607
lp: hmv ALP 1160
lp: hmv (italy) QALP 10170
lp: victor LM 1222
lp: emi RLS 722/1C147 52448-52454M/
    1C047 01553M
lp: turnabout THS 65068-65070
cd: emi CHS 764 7082
cd: testament SBT 1188

sonatina in f WoO 50

london
22 june
1948

78: hmv C 4003/C 7786
lp: emi 1C147 53382-53389
*according to michael gray this work was re-recorded
on tape on 15 september 1951 but not issued*

piano trio no 7 "archduke"

london
13-19
july 1943

holst, violin
pini, cello

hmv unpublished

london
9-11
september
1943

holst, violin
pini, cello

78: hmv C 3362-3366/C 7588-7592 auto
78: hmv (australia) EB 310-314/
    EB 535-539 auto
lp: arabesque (usa) MD 8032
cd: appian APR 5503
cd: pearl GEM 0143

beethoven **cello sonata no 1**

london	piatigorsky, cello	lp: hmv ALP 1345
5-8		lp: hmv (france) FALP 430
october		lp: electrola E 90892/WALP 1345
1954		lp: victor LM 6120
		lp: emi RLS 731/1C153 03454-03455M/
		1C147 53382-53389
		cd: testament SBT 2158

cello sonata no 2

london	piatigorsky, cello	lp: hmv ALP 1346
11-12		lp: hmv (france) FALP 430
october		lp: electrola E 90893/WALP 1346
1954		lp: victor LM 6120
		lp: emi RLS 731/1C153 03454-03455M/
		1C147 53382-53389
		cd: testament SBT 2158

cello sonata no 3

london	piatigorsky, cello	lp: hmv ALP 1346
12-14		lp: hmv (france) FALP 431
october		lp: electrola E 90893/WALP 1346
1954		lp: victor LM 6120
		lp: emi RLS 731/1C153 03454-03455M/
		1C147 53382-53389
		cd: testament SBT 2158

beethoven **cello sonata no 4**

london	piatigorsky, cello	lp: hmv ALP 1347
8-11		lp: hmv (france) FALP 431
october		lp: electrola E 90894/WALP 1347
1954		lp: victor LM 6120
		lp: emi RLS 731/1C153 03454-03455M/
		1C147 53382-53389
		cd: tesrament SBT 2158

cello sonata no 5

london	piatigorsky, cello	lp: hmv ALP 1347
4-5		lp: hmv (france) FALP 432
october		lp: electrola E 90894/WALP 1347
1954		lp: victor LM 6120
		lp: emi RLS 731/1C153 03454-03455M/
		1C147 53382-53389
		cd: testament SBT 2158
		recording completed on 12 october 1954

ARTHUR BLISS (1891-1975)

piano concerto

liverpool	liverpool	78: hmv C 3348-3352/C 7583-7587 auto
12-13	philharmonic	78: hmv (australia) EB 226-229/
january	boult	EB 524-527 auto
1943		lp: world records SH 125
		lp: emi RLS 701/1E177 01378-01380M
		cd: emi CDH 763 8212
		also issued on 78rpm in sweden and india

JOHANNES BRAHMS (1833-1897)

piano concerto no 1

london	philharmonia	45: victor WHMV 1042
3-5	kubelik	lp: hmv ALP 1172
september		lp: hmv (france) FALP 361
1952		lp: hmv (italy) QALP 361/QALP 10103
		lp: electrola E 90085/WALP 1172
		lp: victor LHMV 1042
		lp: angel AHA 10
		lp: emi SLS 5094/1C151 52652-52655/
		1C147 03081-53082M
		lp: turnabout THS 65110
		cd: testament SBT 1041
		THS 65110 incorrectly dated may 1952

berlin	berlin	cd: myto MCD 89005
15 november	philharmonic	
1954	jochum	

turin	rai torino	unpublished radio broadcast
1955	orchestra	
	maazel	

piano concerto no 2

london	philharmonia	78: hmv C 3610-3615/C 7688-7693 auto
29 april-	dobrowen	lp: emi XLP 30093/1C151 52652-52655/
1 may		SLS 5094/1C147 03081-03082/
1947		1C147 53382-53389
		lp: turnabout THS 65071
		cd: piano library PL 263
		cd: history 20.3175.306
		cd: testament SBT 1042

london	bbc symphony	unpublished radio broadcast
15 october	orchestra	
1953	sargent	

brahms **piano sonata no 3**
london
19·20
august
1952

lp: hmv ALP 1358
lp: emi 1C147 53382 53389
cd: testament SBT 1084

variations and fugue on a theme of handel
london
19 may
1941

columbia unpublished
recording incomplete

london
7 july
1942

78: hmv C 3301-3303/C 7563-7565 auto
lp: emi RLS 701/1E177 01378-01380M/
     1C147 53382-53389
cd: appian APR 5503
cd: philips 456 9732
cd: testament SBT 1041
recording completed 18-24 july and 5 august 1942;
also issued on 78rpm in india

ballade op 118 no 3
london
26 june
1931

columbia unpublished

intermezzo op 116 no 4
berlin
24 february
1956

cd: appian APR 7030

intermezzo op 117 no 2
london
20 april
1944

78: hmv C 3406
78: hmv (norway) ZN 525
78: hmv (australia) EB 266
lp: emi RLS 701/1E177 01378-01380M/
     1C147 53382-53389
cd: philips 456 9732
cd: testament SBT 1042

brahms **intermezzo op 118 no 6**
berlin   cd: appian APR 7030
24 february
1956

intermezzo op 119 no 3
london   cd: testament SBT 1042
21 august   *unpublished hmv lp recording*
1952

rhapsody op 79 no 1
berlin   cd: appian APR 7030
24 february
1956

rhapsody op 79 no 2
london   78: hmv C 3406
20 april   78: hmv (norway) ZN 525
1944   78: hmv (australia) EB 266
                                    lp: emi 1C147 53382-53389
                                    cd: testament SBT 1042

viola sonata no 2
london   tertis, viola   hmv unpublished
17-18   *recording completed on 29 may 1945*
february
1945

FREDERIC CHOPIN (1810-1849)

ballade no 4
london
1 april
1946

78: hmv C 3403
lp: emi RLS 701/1E177 01378-01380M/
    1C147 53382-53389
cd: philips 456 9732
cd: testament SBT 1030
also issued on 78rpm in india

berceuse in d flat
london
21 august
1942

hmv unpublished

london
4 september
1942

78: hmv C 3308
78: hmv (finland) TH 16
78: hmv (australia) EB 315
78: hmv (ireland) IPX 173
lp: emi RLS 701/1E177 01378-01380M/
    1C147 53382-53389
cd: appian APR 5503
cd: philips 456 9732
cd: testament SBT 1030

étude op 10 no 3
london
21 june
1945

hmv unpublished

london
3 july
1945

78: hmv C 3433
78: hmv (finland) TH 167
78: hmv (australia) EB 267
78: hmv (ireland) IPX 181
lp: emi RLS 701/1E177 01378-01380M/
    1C147 53382-53389
cd: testament SBT 1030

chopin **étude op 10 no 8**
london
29 december
1934

78: columbia DX 669
78: columbia (australia) DOX 481
lp: emi 1C147 53382-53389
lp: discocorp IGI 333
cd: pearl GEMMCD 9478
cd: testament SBT 1030
cd: naxos 811.0680

étude op 10 no 9
london
16 september
1942

78: hmv C 3345
lp: emi 1C147 53382-53389
cd: appian APR 5503
also issued on 78rpm in sweden and india

london
21 october
1942

hmv unpublished

étude op 25 no 1
london
14 december
1932

78: columbia LX 314
78: columbia (australia) DOX 194
lp: emi RLS 701/1E177 01378-01380M/
      1C147 53382-53389
lp: discocorp IGI 333
cd: pearl GEMMCD 9478
cd: testament SBT 1030
cd: naxos 811.0680

chopin étude op 25 no 2
london
16 september
1942

78: hmv C 3345
lp: emi 1C147 53382-53389
cd: appian APR 5503
also issued on 78rpm in sweden and india

london
21 october
1942

hmv unpublished

étude op 25 no 3
london
29 december
1934

78: columbia DX 669
78: columbia (australia) DOX 481
lp: emi 1C147 63382-53389
lp: discocorp IGI 333
cd: pearl GEMMCD 9478
cd: testament SBT 1030
cd: naxos 811.0680

london
16 september
1942

78: hmv C 3345
lp: emi 1C147 53382-53389
cd: appian APR 5503
also issued on 78rpm in sweden and india

london
21 october
1942

hmv unpublished

fantasy in f minor
london
2 december
1932

78: columbia DX 668-669
lp: emi RLS 701/1E177 01378-01380M/
       1C147 53382-53389
lp: discocorp IGI 333
cd: pearl GEMMCD 9478
cd: philips 456 9732
cd: testament SBT 1030
cd: naxos 811.0680

berlin
23 february
1956

cd: appian APR 7030

chopin **mazurka op 68 no 2**
london   78: hmv C 3509
2 april   lp: emi 1C147 53382-53389
1946   cd: testament SBT 1030
                                        also issued on 78rpm in india

nocturne op 9 no 1
berlin   cd: appian APR 7030
23 february
1956

nocturne op 9 no 2
london   78: hmv C 3345
4 september   lp: emi RLS 701/1E177 01378-01380M/
1942   1C147 53382-53389
                                        also issued on 78rpm in sweden and india

nocturne op 27 no 2
london   78: hmv C 3308
21 august   78: hmv (finland) TH 16
1942   78: hmv (australia) EB 315
                                        78: hmv (ireland) IPX 173
                                        lp: emi 1C147 53382-53389
                                        cd: appian APR 5503
                                        cd: testament SBT 1030
                                        cd: brilliant classics 99228/99230

polonaise no 3
london   78: columbia DX 441
30 november   78: columbia (australia) DOX 350
1932   78: columbia (japan) J 8211
                                        lp: emi RLS 701/1E177 01378-01380M/
                                              1C147 53382-53389
                                        lp: discocorp IGI 333
                                        cd: pearl GEMMCD 9478
                                        cd: testament SBT 1030
                                        cd: naxos 811.0680

chopin polonaise no 6
london
14 december
1932

78: columbia LX 314
78: columbia (australia) DOX 194
lp: emi RLS 701/1E177 01378-01380M/
   1C147 53382-53389
lp: discocorp IGI 333
cd: pearl GEMMCD 9478
cd: philips 456 9732
cd: testament SBT 1030
cd: naxos 811.0680

scherzo no 2
berlin
23 february
1956

cd: appian APR 7030

valse op 42
london
21 june
1945

hmv unpublished

london
3 july
1945

78: hmv C 3433
78: hmv (finland) TH 167
78: hmv (australia) EB 267
78: hmv (ireland) IPX 181
lp: emi RLS 701/1E177 01378-01380M/
   1C147 53382-53389
cd: testament SBT 1030

valse in e minor op posth.
london
2 april
1946

78: hmv C 3509
lp: emi RLS 701/1E177 01378-01380M/
   1C147 53382-53389
cd: testament SBT 1030

FRANCOIS COUPERIN (1668-1733)

le carillon de cythere/ordre xiv

london
22 may
1951

78: hmv C 4119/C 7871
45: hmv 7P 123
45: electrola 7PW 116
45: victor WDM 1654
lp: emi 1C147 53382-53389
also issued on 78rpm in the netherlands

LOUIS-CLAUDE DAQUIN (1694-1772)

le coucou/premier livre de pieces de clavecin

london
2 april
1946

78: hmv C 3509
lp: emi 1C147 53382-53389
cd: appian APR 2000
also issued on 78rpm in india

CLAUDE DEBUSSY (1862-1918)

voiles/préludes livre 1

london	78: hmv B 9561
1 april	lp: emi 1C147 53382-53389
1946	*also issued on 78rpm in australia*

la fille aux cheveux de lin/préludes livre 1

london	78: hmv B 9561
2 april	78: hmv (finland) TG 102
1946	lp: emi 1C147 53382-53389
	also issued on 78rpm in spain, australia and india

la cathédrale engloutie/préludes livre 1

london	hmv unpublished
20 may	
1948	

london	78: hmv B 9757
22 june	lp: emi 1C147 53382-53389
1948	

CESAR FRANCK (1822-1890

prélude, aria et final

london	columbia unpublished
17 june	*recording completed on 26 june and 12 august 1931*
1931	

EDVARD GRIEG (1843-1907)

piano concerto

london	philharmonia	lp: hmv ALP 1643/ASD 272
25-26	menges	lp: capitol G 7191/SG 7191
september		lp: emi SLS 5094/1C151 52652-52655/
1956		CFP 40255/1C053 00154
		lp: quintessence (usa) PC 4034/PMC 7055
		lp: paperback classics (usa) L 9219/SL 9219
		cd: emi CDEMX 2002/CZS 767 7352
		cd: testament SBT 1231

FRANZ JOSEF HAYDN (1732-1809)

piano sonata in c hobXVI/35

london	lp: hmv BLP 1076
19 august	lp: emi XLP 30053/1C147 53382-53389
1952	

piano sonata in d hobXVI/37

london	78: hmv C 3494
1-2	lp: emi 1C147 53382-53389
april	lp: arabesque (usa) MD 8032
1946	cd: pearl GEM 0038
	also issued on 78rpm in india

FRANZ LISZT (1811-1886)

hungarian fantasia for piano and orchestra

london	philharmonia	78: hmv C 3761-3762/C 7688-7689 auto
27 april	susskind	45: hmv 7EP 7132
1948		lp: emi RLS 701/1E177 01378-01380M/
		SLS 5094/1C151 52652-52655/
		1C147 53382-53389
		lp: world records SH 125
		lp: turnabout THS 65108
		cd: emi CDH 763 8212
		cd: testament SBT 1231
		also issued on 78rpm in denmark and india

hungarian rhapsody no 15 "rakoczy"

london	columbia unpublished
6 october	
1932	

london	78: columbia DX 441
16 december	78: columbia (australia) DOX 350
1932	78: columbia (japan) J 8211
	lp: discocorp IGI 333
	lp: bbc records REH 718
	cd: bbc records BBCCD 718
	cd: pearl GEMMCD 9478
	cd: philips 456 9732
	cd: testament SBT 1084
	cd: naxos 811.0680

liszt **au bord d'une source/années de pelerinage**

london   columbia unpublished
29 november
1929

london   78: columbia LX 57
17 july   78: columbia (argentina) 266 318
1930   lp: emi HLM 7093/1C047 06168M
                                          lp: discocorp IGI 333
                                          lp: bbc records REH 718
                                          cd: bbc records BBCCD 718
                                          cd: pearl GEMMCD 9478
                                          cd: philips 456 9732
                                          cd: testament SBT 1084
                                          cd: naxos 811.0680

la leggierezza/études de concert
london   columbia unpublished
29 november
1929

london   78: columbia LX 57
17 july   78: columbia (argentina) 266 318
1930   lp: discocorp IGI 333
                                          lp: bbc records REH 718
                                          cd: bbc records BBCCD 718
                                          cd: pearl GEMMCD 9478
                                          cd: philips 456 9732
                                          cd: naxos 811.0680

GIOVANNI MARTINI (1706-1784)

allegro from sonata in d, arranged by endicott
london   tertis, viola   hmv unpublished
18 february
1945

WOLFGANG AMADEUS MOZART (1756-1791)

piano concerto no 15

london	philharmonia	lp: hmv ALP 1194
7-8	ackermann	lp: hmv (italy) QALP 10167
september		lp: victor LHMV 12
1953		lp: angel AHA 3
		lp: emi RLS 726/1C153 03250-03251M/
		1C147 50183-50184M
		cd: emi CDH 763 7072
		cd: testament SBT 1222

piano concerto no 23

london	philharmonia	lp: hmv ALP 1316
10-11	menges	lp: hmv (italy) QALP 10173
may		lp: electrola E 90129/WALP 1316
1955		lp: emi RLS 726/1C153 03250-03251M/
		1C147 50183-50184M/
		1C147 53382-53389
		cd: emi CDH 763 7072
		cd: testament SBT 1222

piano concerto no 24

london	philharmonia	lp: hmv ALP 1316
11-12	menges	lp: hmv (italy) QALP 10173
may		lp: electrola E 90129/WALP 1316
1955		lp: emi RLS 726/1C153 03250-03251M/
		1C147 50183-50184M
		cd: emi CDH 763 7072
		cd: testament SBT 1222

mozart **piano sonata no 11 k331**

london
2 december
1952

lp: hmv ALP 1194
lp: victor LHMV 12
lp: angel AHA 3
lp: emi XLP 30053/RLS 726/
    1C153 03250-03251M/
    1C147 50183-50184M
cd: testament SBT 1221

piano sonata no 13 k333

london
4 may
1943

cd: philips 456 9732
unpublished hmv 78rpm recording

london
28 august
1956

unpublished radio broadcast

piano sonata no 18 k576

london
9 june
1952

lp: hmv BLP 1076
lp: emi RLS 726/1C153 03250-03251M/
    1C147 53382-53389
cd: testament SBT 1221

DOMENICO SCARLATTI (1685-1757)

sonata in f K 17/L 384

london
20 may
1948

78: hmv C 3768
78: hmv (norway) ZN 556
lp: emi 1C147 53382-53389
cd: appian APR 2000
cd: pearl GEM 0038
also issued on 78rpm in the netherlands

FRANZ SCHUBERT (1797-1828)

piano sonata no 13 d664

london	lp: hmv ALP 1901
23 august	lp: electrola E 80651/WCLP 771
1956	lp: emi XLP 30053/1C147 53382-53389
	cd: testament SBT 1230
	recording completed on 28 august 1956

london	unpublished radio broadcast
28 august	
1956	

piano sonata no 14 d784

london	lp: hmv ALP 1901
3-4	lp: electrola E 80651/WCLP 771
december	lp: victor LHMV 21
1952	lp: angel AHA 3
	lp: emi 1C147 53382-52289
	cd: testament SBT 1230

marche militaire d733

london	columbia unpublished
4 january	
1933	

london	columbia unpublished
24 january	
1933	

ROBERT SCHUMANN (1810-1856)

piano concero

london	philharmonia	lp: hmv ALP 1643/ASD 272
19 september	menges	lp: capitol G 7191/SG 7191
1956		lp: emi SLS 5094/CFP 40255/
		1C151 52652-52655/1C053 00154
		lp: quintessence (usa) PC 4034/PMC 7055
		lp: paperback classics (usa) L 9219/SL 9219
		cd: emi CDEMX 2002/CZS 767 7352
		cd: testament SBT 1231

recording completed on 24 september 1956; excerpts from the recording also issued on hmv 45rpm

carnaval

london	lp: emi HQM 1077/1C147 53382-53389
7-8	lp: angel IC-6045
june	cd: testament SBT 1084
1952	

ALEXANDER SCRIABIN (1872-1915)

piano concerto

london	philharmonia	cd: emi CDH 763 8212
23-25	dobrowen	cd: testament SBT 1232
may		*unpublished hmv 78rpm recording, funded by*
1949		*the maharajah of mysore*

DEODAT DE SEVERAC (1872-1921)

la boite a joujoux/en vacances

london	78: hmv C 3509
2 april	lp: emi 1C147 53382-53389
1946	cd: appian APR 2000
	also issued on 78rpm in india

PIOTR TCHAIKOVSKY (1840-1893)

piano concerto no 1

london	hallé ochestra	78: columbia LX 19-22
30 november	harty	78: columbia (france) LFX 19-22
1929		78: columbia (germany) DWX 1332-1335
		78: columbia (australia) LOX 25-28
		78: columbia (usa) M 141
		lp: discocorp IGI 333
		lp: bbc records REH 718
		cd: bbc records BBCCD 718
		cd: pearl GEMMCD 9478
		cd: italy HTM 90004
		cd: history 20.3175.306
		cd: phonographe PH 5015
		cd: naxos 811.0680
		recording completed on 8 february 1930

london	philharmonia	78: hmv C 3996-3999/C 7776-7779 auto
26-28	dobrowen	78: hmv (italy) S 10578-10580
may		78: electrola EH 1365-1368
1949		45: victor WHMV 1028
		lp: hmv CLP 1001
		lp: hmv (italy) QCLP 12004
		lp: electrola E 80043/WCLP 1001
		lp: victor LHMV 1028
		lp: emi SLS 5094/1C151 52653-52655/
		1C053 01402M
		lp: turnabout THS 65108
		cd: emi CHS 764 8552
		cd: piano library PL 263
		cd: testament SBT 1232
		also issued on 78 rpm in the netherlands and
		switzerland; excerpts from the recording also
		issued on various hmv 45 rpm discs

kansas city	kansas city	unpublished radio broadcast
29-30	philharmonic	
january	schweiger	
1952		

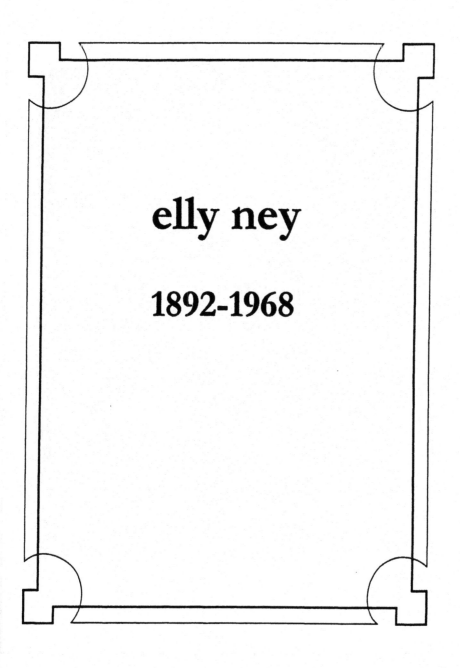

elly ney

1892-1968

JOHANN SEBASTIAN BACH (1685-1750)

ertöt' uns durch dein' güte/chorale from cantata 22, arrangement
nürnberg   lp: colosseum COM 526/COST 526
12 october
1962

prelude and fugue in c bwv 870/wohltemperiertes klavier book I
nürnberg   lp: colosseum COM 526/COST 526
12 october
1962

prelude and fugue in b flat bwv 890/wohltemperiertes klavier book II
new york   78: brunswick B62/B63
5 august
1924

new york   78: brunswick 13392/13393
22 october
1924

nürnberg   lp: colosseum COM 526/COST 526
12 october
1962

LUDWIG VAN BEETHOVEN (1770-1827)

piano concerto no 2

berlin	orchestra	78: electrola DB 4503-4506
23 november	zaun	cd: biddulph BID 82045
1937		

piano concerto no 3

vienna	vienna	cd: refrain (japan) MADR 206
12 april	philharmonic	*reichsrundfunk recording*
1944	böhm	

nürnberg	nürnberg	lp: colosseum COM 505/COST 505
21 january	symphony	cd: colosseum COL 90152
1961	hoogstraten	

piano concerto no 4

nürnberg	nürnberg	lp: colosseum COM 506/COST 506
january	symphony	cd: colosseum COL 90152
1961	hoogstaten	

beethoven **piano concerto no 5 "emperor"**

vienna	vienna	lp: urania URLP 7150/URRS 7-10
1944	philharmonic	cd: stradivarius DAT 12305
	böhm	cd: refrain (japan) MADR 206
		cd: tahra TAH 335-336/TAH 444-446
		reichsrundfunk recording; stradivarius incorrectly dated 1956

berlin	berlin	cd: tahra TAH 192-193
13 october	philharmonic	*reichsrundfunk recording*
1944	abendroth	

nürnberg	nürnberg	lp: colosseum COM 502/COST 502
13-14	symphony	cd: colosseum COL 90192
july	hoogstraten	*lp edition contains spoken introduction by elly ney*
1960		

cello sonata no 1, first movement

berlin	hoelscher, cello	unpublished radio broadcast
25 march		*reichsrundfunk recording; date given is probably*
1944		*date on which the tapes were edited*

cello sonata no 2, first movement

berlin	hoelscher, cello	unpublished radio broadcast
25 march		*reichsrundfunk recording; date given is probably*
1944		*date on which the tapes were edited*

cello sonata no 3

munich	hoelscher, cello	lp: telefunken BLE 14087
14 june		cd: bayer BR 200.035
1955		*bavarian radio recording*

cello sonata no 4

munich	hoelscher, cello	lp: telefunken BLE 14087
28 april		cd: bayer BR 200.035
1964		*bavarian radio recording*

beethoven **cello sonata no 5**

munich	hoelscher, cello	lp: telefunken BLE 14097
14 june		cd: bayer BR 200.035
1955		*bavarian radio recording*

12 variations on a theme from handel's judas maccabaeus for cello and piano

munich	hoelscher, cello	lp: telefunken BLE 14097
14 june		*bavarian radio recording*
1955		

7 variations on mozart's bei männern welche liebe fühlen for cello and piano

munich	hoelscher, cello	lp: relefunken BLE 14087
14 june		*bavarian radio recording*
1955		

12 variations on mozart's ein mädchen oder weibchen for cello and piano

munich	hoelscher, cello	lp: telefunken BLE 14097
14 june		*bavarian radio recording*
1955		

piano sonata no 4

berlin	78: electrola DB 4582-4585
7 june	cd: biddulph LHW 033
1938	

nürnberg	lp: colosseum COM 518/COST 518
9 march	cd: colosseum COL 90182
1967	

beethoven **piano sonata no 8 "pathétique"**

hannover	lp: dg LPEM 19 084
18-22	
december	
1956	

nürnberg	lp: colosseum COM 521/COST 521
6 march	cd: colosseum COL 90182
1967	

piano sonata no 8, second movement

berlin	78: electrola DB 4460
october	cd: biddulph LHW 033
1936	

piano sonata no 8, third movement

berlin	unpublished radio broadcast
1943-1944	*reichsrundfunk recording*

piano sonata no 12 "funeral march"

nürnberg	lp: colosseum COM 519/COST 519
7 may	cd: colosseum COL 90182
1965	*first movement*
	45: colosseum COM 1015

piano sonata no 14 "moonlight"

berlin	unpublished radio broadcast
1943-1944	*reichsrundfunk recording*

hannover	lp: dg LPEM 19 085/2872 809/478 122
19 december	
1956	

nürnberg	lp: colosseum COM 518/COST 518
9 march	cd: colosseum COL 90212
1967	

piano sonata no 17 "tempest"

nürnberg	lp: colosseum COM 520/COST 520
20 june	cd: colosseum COL 90212
1964	

beethoven **piano sonata no 18**

nürnberg	lp: colosseum COM 520/COST 520
20 june	cd: colosseum COL 90222
1964	

piano sonata no 21 "waldstein"

dortmund	cd: bayer BR 200.048
1952	*rehearsal performance*

nürnberg	lp: colosseum COM 503/COST 503
16 july	cd: colosseum COL 90212
1960	

piano sonata no 21, first movement

berlin	unpublished radio broadcast
27 november	*reichsrundfunk recording*
1944	

piano sonata no 23 "appassionata"

berlin	cd: melodram MEL 18015
28 october	*sender freies berlin*
1952	

hannover	lp: dg LPEM 19 085/478 122
20-22	
december	
1956	

nürnberg	lp: colosseum COM 519/COST 519
7 may	cd: colosseum COL 90192
1965	

beethoven **piano sonata no 29, third movement**

nürnberg   lp: colosseum COM 527/COST 527
1968   cd: colosseum COL 90222

piano sonata no 30

nürnberg   lp: colosseum COM 507/COST 507
1962   cd: colosseum COL 90122

piano sonata no 31

hannover   lp: dg LPEM 19 084/2872 809
21-22
december
1956

nürnberg   lp: colosseum COM 526/COST 526
12 october   cd: colosseum awaiting publication
1962

piano sonata no 32

berlin   78: electrola DB 4476-4479
6 may   lp: electrola E 80479
1936   cd: biddulph LHW 033
                             cd: history 20.3172 306
                             recording completed on 27 may 1936

dortmund   lp: somerset 591
1952   cd: bayer BR 200.048
                             rehearsal performance

1958   lp: electrola E 80479

nürnberg   lp: colosseum COM 527/COM 616/
july   COST 527/COST 616
1964   cd: colosseum COL 90122

beethoven **andante favori in f**

berlin	78: electrola DB 4676
23 november	lp: electrola E 60564
1937	cd: biddulph LHW 033
	re-reccorded on 16 february 1938

nürnberg	45: colosseum COM 1014
23 may	cd: colosseum COL 90132
1965	*recorded on graf fortepiano*

bagatelle in a minor "für elise"

nürnberg	45: colosseum COM 1014
15-16	cd: colosseum COL 90132
july	*recorded on graf fortepiano*
1960	

nürnberg	45: colosseum COM 1005
23 may	
1965	

écossaises, arranged by d'albert

new york	78: brunswick 9305/9306/15036
november	
1922	

new york	78: brunswick 24018/24019
18 july	
1927	

nürnberg	45: colosseum COM 1005
15-16	cd: colosseum COL 90222
july	
1960	

beethoven **rondo a capriccio in g "rage over a lost penny"**

| nürnberg 15-16 july 1960 | 45: colosseum COM 1005 |
| | cd: colosseum COL 90222 |

6 variations on paisiello's nel cor piu non mi sento

berlin 6 may 1936	78: electrola DB 4479
	cd: biddulph LHW 033
	cd: piano library PL 329
	recording completed on 21 april 1938

| nürnberg 15-16 july 1960 | 45: colosseum COM 1005 |

nürnberg 23 may 1965	45: colosseum COM 1014
	cd: colosseum COL 90132
	recorded on graf fortepiano

6 variations in f on an original theme

| nürnberg 16 july 1960 | lp: colosseum COM 503/COST 503 |
| | cd: colosseum COL 90222 |

32 variations in c minor on an original theme woO 80

| nürnberg 16 july 1960 | lp: colosseum COM 503/COST 503 |
| | cd: colosseum COL 90222 |

piano trio no 3, third movement

| berlin 14 may 1937 | strub, violin hoelscher, cello | 78: electrola DB 4590 |

beethoven **piano trio no 5 "ghost"**

berlin	strub, violin	78: electrola DB 4587-4590
14 may	hoelscher, cello	lp: electrola E 60564
1937		

heiligenstadt testament

berlin	*elly ney reads*	78: electrola DB 4460
27 may	*in german*	cd: biddulph LHW 033
1936		

nürnberg	*elly ney reads*	45: colosseum COM 1015
date not	*in german*	
confirmed		

LUIGI BOCCHERINI (1743-1805)

rondo, arranged for cello and piano by bazelaire

berlin	hoelscher, cello	78: electrola EG 3041
2 may		
1935		

JOHANNES BRAHMS (1833-1897)

piano concerto no 2

berlin	berlin	78: grammophon 67566-67571
1-5	philharmonic	78: ultraphon 19027-19032
june	fiedler	lp: decca (usa) DL 9536
1939		lp: dg 88 010
		cd: piano library PL 329
		cd: refrain (japan) PMCD 4
		cd: biddulph WHL 003-004
		second movement
		cd: dg 459 0022/459 0652
		recording completed on 29 april 1940 with an unspecified conductor

leipzig	gewandhaus-	cd: melodram MEL 18015
3 march	orchester	
1955	konwitschny	

piano concerto no 2, fourth movement

luxembourg	orchestra	unpublished radio broadcast
30 april	hoogstraten	*reichsrundfunk recording*
1944		

piano sonata no 3

nürnberg		lp: colosseum COM 522/COST 522
date not		cd: colosseum awaiting publication
confirmed		

hungarian dance no 2 in d minor, arrangement

new york	78: brunswick 7233/15021
january	
1922	

new york	78: brunswick 24027/24028/24029
19 july	
1927	

brahms **o wie selig seid ihr doch/11 chorale preludes**

nürnberg
12 october
1962

lp: colosseum COM 526/COST 526

intermezzo op 76 no 3
berlin
20 september
1937

78: electrola DA 4438
45: electrola E 40070/7EGW 11-8375

intermezzo op 117 no 1
berlin
20 september
1937

78: electrola DB 4426
45: electrola E 40070/7EGW 11-8375

nürnberg
date not
confirmed

lp: colosseum COM 522/COST 522
cd: colosseum awaiting publication

intermezzo op 118 no 6
nürnberg
date not
confirmed

lp: colosseum COM 522/COST 522
cd: colosseum awaiting publication

rhapsody op 119 no 4
berlin
20 september
1937

78: electrola DA 4438
45: electrola E 40070/7EGW 11-8375

nürnberg
12 october
1962

lp: colosseum COM 526/COST 526

brahms romance op 118 no 5

nürnberg
date not
confirmed

lp: colosseum COM 522/COST 522
cd: colosseum awaiting publication

waltz op 39 no 15

berlin
20 september
1937

78: electrola DA 4438
45: electrola E 40070/7EGW 11-8375

song transcriptions: guten abend gut' nacht; sandmännchen

nürnberg
24 september
1963

lp: colosseum COM 1008

piano trio no 1

| berlin | strub, violin | 78: grammophon 27316-27319 |
| 1939 | hoelscher, cello | cd: classical record ACR 39 |

TERESA CARRENO (1853-1917)

petite valse

new york
6 august
1924

78: brunswick B79/B80/B81

new york
22 october
1924

78: brunswick 13989

new york
22 october
1924

78: brunswick 13999/14000/15094
second version recorded on this date

new york
18 july
1927

78: brunswick 24014/24015

FREDERIC CHOPIN (1810-1849)

ballade no 3
nürnberg   lp: colosseum COM 2003/COST 2003
date not
confirmed

étude op 10 no 3
new york   78: brunswick 10042
3 march
1923

new york   78: brunswick 10070/10071
7 march
1923

new york   78: brunswick 10157/50032
21 march
1923

fantasy in f minor
nürnberg   lp: colosseum COM 2003/COST 2003
date not
confirmed

nocturne op 15 no 2
nürnberg   lp: colosseum COM 2003/COST 2003
date not
confirmed

chopin nocturne op 37 no 2
nürnberg   lp: colosseum COM 2003/COST 2003
date not
confirmed

nocturne op 48 no 1
nürnberg   lp: colosseum COM 2003/COST 2003
date not
confirmed

nocturne op 48 no 2
new york   78: brunswick 7381/15021
february
1922

new york   78: brunswick 24030/24031
19 july
1927

CLAUDE DEBUSSY (1862-1918)

feux d'artifice/préludes livre II
new york   78: brunswick B64
5 august
1924

new york   78: brunswick B77/B78
6 august
1924

new york   78: brunswick 13997/13998/15094
22 october
1924

new york   78: brunswick 24011/24012/24013
18 july
1927

THEODOR GAUSMANN

variations on the folksong "weisst du wieviel sternlein steh'n?"
berlin   unpublished radio broadcast
1943-1944   *reichsrundfunk recording*

CHRISTOPH WILLIBALD GLUCK (1714-1787)

dance of the blessed spirits from orfeo ed euridice, arranged for cello and piano by grünfeld
berlin   hoelscher, cello   78: electrola EG 3041
2 may
1935

dance of the blessed spirits from orfeo ed euridice, arranged for piano
nürnberg   45: colosseum COM 2002
6 february
1961

LOUIS GOTTSCHALK (1829-1869)

pasquinade caprice
new york   78: brunswick 11392/11393/11394
24 september
1923

new york   78: brunswick 11530/11531
4 october
1923

PAUL GRAENER (1872-1944)

kein hälmlein wächst auf erden, arrangement
nürnberg   lp: colosseum COM 1008
24 september
1963

FRANZ JOSEF HAYDN (1732-1809)

rondo all' ongarese/piano trio no 25
berlin   strub, violin   78: grammophon 15090/67071
1939   hoelscher, cello   78: decca CA 8214

FRANZ LISZT (1811-1886)

hungarian rhapsody no 8
1906   welte piano roll

new york   78: brunswick 10039/10040/10041
3 march
1923

new york   78: brunswick 10072
7 march
1923

new york   78: brunswick 10154/10155/10156/50032
21 march
1923

liszt **hungarian rhapsody no 14, first part**
new york   78: brunswick XB55/XB56/XB57/XB58
5 august
1924

hungarian rhapsody no 14, second part
new york   78: brunswick XB59/XB60/XB61
5 august
1924

new york   78: brunswick XB71/XB72
6 august
1924

valse caprice in a minor/soirées de vienne
new york   78: brunswick 7579/15024
february
1922

new york   78: brunswick 24021/24022/24023
19 july
1927

EDWARD MACDOWELL (1860-1908)

polonaise in e minor/12 virtuoso études

new york 4 october 1923	78: brunswick 11534/11535/11536
new york 4 august 1924	78: brunswick B43/B44/B47

valse triste/12 virtuoso études

new york 24 september 1923	78: brunswick 11395/11396/11397
new york 4 october 1923	78: brunswick 11532/11533
new york 4 august 1924	78: brunswick B48/B49

FELIX MENDELSSOHN-BARTHOLDY (1809-1847)

lied ohne worte op 19 no 1
nürnberg   lp: colosseum COM 521/COST 521
6 march
1967

lied ohne worte op 62 no 3 "trauermarsch"
nürnberg   lp: colosseum COM 521/COST 521
6 march
1967

lied ohne worte op 62 no 6 "frühlingslied"
nürnberg   lp: colosseum COM 521/COST 521
6 march
1967

lied ohne worte op 67 no 4 "spinnerlied"
new york   78: brunswick 9574/9575/15036
december
1922

new york   78: brunswick 24016/24017
18 july
1927

lied ohne worte op 102 no 5 "kinderstück"
nürnberg   lp: colosseum COM 1008
24 september
1963

nürnberg   lp: colosseum COM 521/COST 521
6 march
1967

WOLFGANG AMADEUS MOZART (1756-1791)

piano concerto no 15

berlin   orchestra   78: electrola DB 4435-4437/
1 october   hoogstraten   DB 8071-8073 auto
1935   78: victor M 365
                                        cd: biddulph BID 82045
                                        recording completed on 21 november 1935

piano sonata no 10 k330

nürnberg   lp: colosseum COM 507/COST 507
date not
confirmed

piano sonata no 11 k331

nürnberg   lp: colosseum COM 616/COST 616
july   lp: somerset 591
1964

andantino k236

nürnberg   lp: colosseum COM 1008
date not
confirmed

rondo in a minor k511

berlin   78: electrola DB 4620
20 september   *re-recorded on 10 february 1938*
1937

nürnberg   45: colosseum COM 2002
6 february
1961

agnus dei from litaniae laurentanae, arrangement

nürnberg   lp: colosseum COM 1008
24 september
1963

MAX REGER (1873-1916)

burleske und menuett /suite in a minor for violin and piano
berlin	strub, violin	78: electrola EH 969
1935		cd: classical record ACR 39

lyrisches andante for strings, arranged for violin and piano
berlin	strub, violin	78: electrola EH 969
1935		cd: classical record ACR 39

FRANZ SCHUBERT (1797-1828)

wanderer fantasy
berlin
1941

78: grammophon 67876-67878
cd: piano library PL 329
cd: history 20.3172 306

nürnberg
1964

lp: colosseum COM 523/COST 523
cd: colosseum COL 90162

sonata rondo, unspecified
new york
6 august
1924

78: brunswick XB75/XB76

impromptu d899 no 3
nürnberg
6 february
1961

45: colosseum COM 2002

impromptu d899 no 4
nürnberg
1964

lp: colosseum COM 523/COST 523

impromptu d935 no 3
berlin
1 december
1944

unpublished radio broadcast
reichsrundfunk recording

impromptu d935 no 4
new york
6 august
1924

78: brunswick XB73/XB74

nürnberg
1964

lp: colosseum COM 523/COST 523

schubert **moment musical no 2**
nürnberg   lp: colosseum COM 523/COST 523
1964

moment musical no 3
new york   78: brunswick 9303/9304/15036
november
1922

new york   78: brunswick 9574/9575/15036
december
1922

new york   78: brunswick 24016/24017
18 july
1927

nürnberg   lp: colosseum COM 523/COST 523
1964

moment musical no 4
berlin   78: electrola DB 4432
1935

nürnberg   lp: colosseum COM 523/COST 523
1964

15 deutsche tänze
berlin   78: grammophon 67878
1941

nürnberg   45: colosseum COM 2002
6 february
1961

schubert **cello sonata in a "arpeggione"**

berlin	hoelscher, cello	78: electrola EH 929-921
2 may		78: victor (japan) JH 22-23
1935		cd: classical record ACR 39

piano trio no 1

berlin	strub, violin	78: grammophon 57045-57048
1939	hoelscher, cello	78: decca X 157-160

piano trio no 2, third movement

berlin	strub, violin	78: electrola DB 4537
16 may	hoelscher, cello	
1938		

piano quintet in a "trout"

berlin	strub string	78: electrola DB 4533-4537
16 may	quartet	lp: electrola E 80838
1938		*recording completed on 7 june 1938*

frühlingsglaube, song arranged for solo piano by liszt

new york	78: brunswick 10043/10044/10045
3 march	
1923	

new york	78: brunswick B45/B46
4 august	
1924	

new york	78: brunswick 13994/13995
22 october	
1924	

nürnberg	lp: colosseum COM 1008
24 september	
1963	

schubert **goldene abendsonne, song arranged for solo piano by liszt**
nürnberg   lp: colosseum COM 1008
24 september
1963

horch horch die lerch', song arranged for solo piano by liszt
new york   78: brunswick 7581/15024
february
1922 ·

new york   78: brunswick 24024/24025/24026
19 july
1927

wiegenlied, song arranged for solo piano by liszt
nürnberg   lp: colosseum COM 1008
24 september
1963

ROBERT SCHUMANN (1810-1856)

études symphoniques
nürnberg
1962

lp: colosseum COM 508/COST 508
cd: colosseum COL 90162

warum?/fantasiestücke
nürnberg
1962

lp: colosseum COM 508/COST 508

kinderszenen
berlin
12 march
1937

78: electrola DB 4471-4472
lp: electrola E 60048
cd: classical record ACR 39

träumerei/kinderszenen
nürnberg
24 september
1963

lp: colosseum COM 1008

novelette no 1
nürnberg
1962

lp: colosseum COM 508/COST 508

schnitterliedchen/album für die jugend
nürnberg
1962

lp: colosseum COM 508/COST 508

piano quartet in e flat

berlin	strub, violin	78: grammophon 15087-15090
1939	trampler, viola	78: decca CA 8213-8216
	hoelscher, cello	

piano quintet in e flat

berlin	hoffmann	unpublished radio broadcast
25 september	string quartet	*reichsrundfunk recording; date given is probably*
1944		*date on which the tapes were edited*

RICHARD STRAUSS (1864-1949)

burleske for piano and orchestra

berlin	staatskapelle	78: electrola DB 4424-4425
1932	hoogstraten	78: victor 11744-11745
		lp: electrola E 60048
		cd: biddulph BID 82045
		first gramophone recording of the work

ELLY NEY SPEAKS

elly ney spricht: wie ich zu beethoven kam

undated	*elly ney speaks*	cd: tahra TAH 192-193
	in german	*see also entries under beethoven heilgenstadt*
		testament and beethoven piano concerto no 5

Music and Books published by Travis & Emery Music Bookshop:

Anon.: Hymnarium Sarisburiense, cum Rubricis et Notis Musicis.

Agricola, Johann Friedrich from Tosi: Anleitung zur Singkunst.

Bach, C.P.E.: edited W. Emery: Nekrolog or Obituary Notice of J.S. Bach

Bateson, Naomi Judith: Alcock of Salisbury

Bathe, William: A Briefe Introduction to the Skill of Song (c.1587)

Bax, Arnold: Symphony #5, Arranged for Piano Four Hands by Walter Emery

Burney, Charles: The Present State of Music in France and Italy (1771)

Burney, Charles: The Present State of Music in Germany, Netherlands... (1773)

Burney, Charles: An Account of the Musical Performances ... Handel (1784)

Burney, Karl: Nachricht von Georg Friedrich Handel's Lebensumstanden (1784)

Burns, Robert: The Caledonian Musical Museum ... Best Scotch Songs (1810)

Cobbett, W.W.: Cobbett's Cyclopedic Survey of Chamber Music. (2 vols.)

Corrette, Michel: Le Maitre de Clavecin (1753)

Crimp, Bryan: Dear Mr. Rosenthal ... Dear Mr. Gaisberg ...

Crimp, Bryan: Solo: The Biography of Solomon

d'Indy, Vincent: Beethoven: Biographie Critique (in French, 1911)

d'Indy, Vincent: Beethoven: A Critical Biography (in English, 1912)

d'Indy, Vincent: César Franck (in French, 1910)

Fischhof, Joseph: Versuch einer Geschichte des Clavierbaues (1853).

Frescobaldi, Girolamo: D'Arie Musicali per Cantarsi. Primo & Secondo Libro.

Geminiani, Francesco: The Art of Playing the Violin (1751)

Handel; Purcell; Boyce et al: Calliope or English Harmony: Vol. First. (1746)

Häuser: Musikalisches Lexikon. 2 vols in one.

Hawkins, John: General History of the Science & Practice of Music (5 vols. 1776)

Herbert-Caesari, Edgar: The Science and Sensations of Vocal Tone

Herbert-Caesari, Edgar: Vocal Truth

Hopkins and Rimboult: The Organ. Its History and Construction.

Hunt, John: Adam to Webern: the recordings of von Karajan

Hunt, John: several discographies – see separate list.

Isaacs, Lewis: Hänsel and Gretel. A Guide to Humperdinck's Opera.

Isaacs, Lewis: Königskinder (Royal Children) A Guide to Humperdinck's Opera.

Kastner: Manuel Général de Musique Militaire

Lacassagne, M. l'Abbé Joseph : Traité Général des élémens du Chant.

Lascelles (née Catley), Anne: The Life of Miss Anne Catley.

Mainwaring, John: Memoirs of the Life of the Late George Frederic Handel

Malcolm, Alexander: A Treaty of Music: Speculative, Practical and Historical

Marx, Adolph Bernhard: Die Kunst des Gesanges, Theoretisch-Practisch (1826)

May, Florence: The Life of Brahms (2nd edition)

May, Florence: The Girlhood Of Clara Schumann: Clara Wieck And Her Time.

Mellers, Wilfrid: Angels of the Night: Popular Female Singers of Our Time

Mellers, Wilfrid: Bach and the Dance of God

Mellers, Wilfrid: Beethoven and the Voice of God

Mellers, Wilfrid: Caliban Reborn - Renewal in Twentieth Century Music

Music and Books published by Travis & Emery Music Bookshop:

Mellers, Wilfrid: François Couperin and the French Classical Tradition
Mellers, Wilfrid: Harmonious Meeting
Mellers, Wilfrid: Le Jardin Retrouvé, The Music of Frederic Mompou
Mellers, Wilfrid: Music and Society, England and the European Tradition
Mellers, Wilfrid: Music in a New Found Land: ... ... American Music
Mellers, Wilfrid: Romanticism and the Twentieth Century (from 1800)
Mellers, Wilfrid: The Masks of Orpheus: ...... the Story of European Music.
Mellers, Wilfrid: The Sonata Principle (from c. 1750)
Mellers, Wilfrid: Vaughan Williams and the Vision of Albion
Panchianio, Cattuffio: Rutzvanscad Il Giovine (1737)
Pearce, Charles: Sims Reeves, Fifty Years of Music in England.
Pettitt, Stephen: Philharmonia Orchestra: Complete Discography (1987)
Playford, John: An Introduction to the Skill of Musick (1674)
Purcell, Henry et al: Harmonia Sacra ... The First Book, (1726)
Purcell, Henry et al: Harmonia Sacra ... Book II (1726)
Quantz, Johann: Versuch einer Anweisung die Flöte traversiere zu spielen.
Rameau, Jean-Philippe: Code de Musique Pratique, ou Methodes (1760)
Rastall, Richard: The Notation of Western Music.
Rimbault, Edward: The Pianoforte, Its Origins, Progress, and Construction.
Rousseau, Jean Jacques: Dictionnaire de Musique
Rubinstein, Anton : Guide to the proper use of the Pianoforte Pedals.
Sainsbury, John S.: Dictionary of Musicians. Vol. 1. (1825). 2 vols.
Serré de Rieux, Jean de : Les dons des Enfans de Latone
Simpson, Christopher: A Compendium of Practical Musick in Five Parts
Spohr, Louis: Autobiography
Spohr, Louis: Grand Violin School
Tans'ur, William: A New Musical Grammar; or The Harmonical Spectator
Terry, Charles Sanford: John Christian Bach (Johann Christian Bach) (1929)
Terry, Charles Sanford: J.S. Bach's Original Hymn-Tunes for Congregational Use
Terry, Charles Sanford: Four-Part Chorals of J.S. Bach. (German & English)
Terry, Charles Sanford: Joh. Seb. Bach. Cantata Texts, Sacred and Secular.
Terry, Charles Sanford: The Origins of the Family of Bach Musicians.
Tosi, Pierfrancesco: Opinioni de' Cantori Antichi, e Moderni (1723)
Van der Straeten, Edmund: History of the Violoncello, The Viol da Gamba ...
Van der Straeten, Edmund: History of the Violin, Its Ancestors... (2 vols.)
Waltern: Musikalisches Lexicon
Walther, J. G.: Musicalisches Lexikon ober Musicalische Bibliothec

Travis & Emery Music Bookshop
17 Cecil Court, London, WC2N 4EZ, United Kingdom.
Tel. (+44) 20 7240 2129

© Travis & Emery 2009

Discographies by Travis & Emery:

Discographies by John Hunt.

1987: 978-1-906857-14-1: From Adam to Webern: the Recordings of von Karajan.

1991: 978-0-951026-83-0: 3 Italian Conductors and 7 Viennese Sopranos: 10 Discographies: Arturo Toscanini, Guido Cantelli, Carlo Maria Giulini, Elisabeth Schwarzkopf, Irmgard Seefried, Elisabeth Gruemmer, Sena Jurinac, Hilde Gueden, Lisa Della Casa, Rita Streich.

1992: 978-0-951026-85-4: Mid-Century Conductors and More Viennese Singers: 10 Discographies: Karl Boehm, Victor De Sabata, Hans Knappertsbusch, Tullio Serafin, Clemens Krauss, Anton Dermota, Leonie Rysanek, Eberhard Waechter, Maria Reining, Erich Kunz.

1993: 978-0-951026-87-8: More 20th Century Conductors: 7 Discographies: Eugen Jochum, Ferenc Fricsay, Carl Schuricht, Felix Weingartner, Josef Krips, Otto Klemperer, Erich Kleiber.

1994: 978-0-951026-88-5: Giants of the Keyboard: 6 Discographies: Wilhelm Kempff, Walter Gieseking, Edwin Fischer, Clara Haskil, Wilhelm Backhaus, Artur Schnabel.

1994: 978-0-951026-89-2: Six Wagnerian Sopranos: 6 Discographies: Frieda Leider, Kirsten Flagstad, Astrid Varnay, Martha Moedl, Birgit Nilsson, Gwyneth Jones.

1995: 978-0-952582-70-0: Musical Knights: 6 Discographies: Henry Wood, Thomas Beecham, Adrian Boult, John Barbirolli, Reginald Goodall, Malcolm Sargent.

1995: 978-0-952582-71-7: A Notable Quartet: 4 Discographies: Gundula Janowitz, Christa Ludwig, Nicolai Gedda, Dietrich Fischer-Dieskau.

1996: 978-0-952582-72-4: The Post-War German Tradition: 5 Discographies: Rudolf Kempe, Joseph Keilberth, Wolfgang Sawallisch, Rafael Kubelik, Andre Cluytens.

1996: 978-0-952582-73-1: Teachers and Pupils: 7 Discographies: Elisabeth Schwarzkopf, Maria Ivoguen, Maria Cebotari, Meta Seinemeyer, Ljuba Welitsch, Rita Streich, Erna Berger.

1996: 978-0-952582-77-9: Tenors in a Lyric Tradition: 3 Discographies: Peter Anders, Walther Ludwig, Fritz Wunderlich.

1997: 978-0-952582-78-6: The Lyric Baritone: 5 Discographies: Hans Reinmar, Gerhard Huesch, Josef Metternich, Hermann Uhde, Eberhard Waechter.

1997: 978-0-952582-79-3: Hungarians in Exile: 3 Discographies: Fritz Reiner, Antal Dorati, George Szell.

1997: 978-1-901395-00-6: The Art of the Diva: 3 Discographies: Claudia Muzio, Maria Callas, Magda Olivero.

1997: 978-1-901395-01-3: Metropolitan Sopranos: 4 Discographies: Rosa Ponselle, Eleanor Steber, Zinka Milanov, Leontyne Price.

1997: 978-1-901395-02-0: Back From The Shadows: 4 Discographies: Willem Mengelberg, Dimitri Mitropoulos, Hermann Abendroth, Eduard Van Beinum.

1997: 978-1-901395-03-7: More Musical Knights: 4 Discographies: Hamilton Harty, Charles Mackerras, Simon Rattle, John Pritchard.

1998: 978-1-901395-94-5: Conductors On The Yellow Label: 8 Discographies: Fritz Lehmann, Ferdinand Leitner, Ferenc Fricsay, Eugen Jochum, Leopold Ludwig, Artur Rother, Franz Konwitschny, Igor Markevitch.

1998: 978-1-901395-95-2: More Giants of the Keyboard: 5 Discographies: Claudio Arrau, Gyorgy Cziffra, Vladimir Horowitz, Dinu Lipatti, Artur Rubinstein.

1998: 978-1-901395-96-9: Mezzo and Contraltos: 5 Discographies: Janet Baker, Margarete Klose, Kathleen Ferrier, Giulietta Simionato, Elisabeth Hoengen.

1999: 978-1-901395-97-6: The Furtwaengler Sound Sixth Edition: Discography and Concert Listing.

1999: 978-1-901395-98-3: The Great Dictators: 3 Discographies: Evgeny Mravinsky, Artur Rodzinski, Sergiu Celibidache.

1999: 978-1-901395-99-0: Sviatoslav Richter: Pianist of the Century: Discography.

2000: 978-1-901395-04-4: Philharmonic Autocrat 1: Discography of: Herbert Von Karajan [Third Edition].

2000: 978-1-901395-05-1: Wiener Philharmoniker 1 - Vienna Philharmonic and Vienna State Opera Orchestras: Discography Part 1 1905-1954.

2000: 978-1-901395-06-8: Wiener Philharmoniker 2 - Vienna Philharmonic and Vienna State Opera Orchestras: Discography Part 2 1954-1989.

2001: 978-1-901395-07-5: Gramophone Stalwarts: 3 Separate Discographies: Bruno Walter, Erich Leinsdorf, Georg Solti.

2001: 978-1-901395-08-2: Singers of the Third Reich: 5 Discographies: Helge Roswaenge, Tiana Lemnitz, Franz Voelker, Maria Mueller, Max Lorenz.

2001: 978-1-901395-09-9: Philharmonic Autocrat 2: Concert Register of Herbert Von Karajan Second Edition.

2002: 978-1-901395-10-5: Sächsische Staatskapelle Dresden: Complete Discography.

2002: 978-1-901395-11-2: Carlo Maria Giulini: Discography and Concert Register.

2002: 978-1-901395-12-9: Pianists For The Connoisseur: 6 Discographies: Arturo Benedetti Michelangeli, Alfred Cortot, Alexis Weissenberg, Clifford Curzon, Solomon, Elly Ney.

2003: 978-1-901395-14-3: Singers on the Yellow Label: 7 Discographies: Maria Stader, Elfriede Troetschel, Annelies Kupper, Wolfgang Windgassen, Ernst Haefliger, Josef Greindl, Kim Borg.

2003: 978-1-901395-15-0: A Gallic Trio: 3 Discographies: Charles Muench, Paul Paray, Pierre Monteux.

2004: 978-1-901395-16-7: Antal Dorati 1906-1988: Discography and Concert Register.

2004: 978-1-901395-17-4: Columbia 33CX Label Discography.

2004: 978-1-901395-18-1: Great Violinists: 3 Discographies: David Oistrakh, Wolfgang Schneiderhan, Arthur Grumiaux.

2006: 978-1-901395-19-8: Leopold Stokowski: Second Edition of the Discography.

2006: 978-1-901395-20-4: Wagner Im Festspielhaus: Discography of the Bayreuth Festival.

2006: 978-1-901395-21-1: Her Master's Voice: Concert Register and Discography of Dame Elisabeth Schwarzkopf [Third Edition].

2007: 978-1-901395-22-8: Hans Knappertsbusch: Kna: Concert Register and Discography of Hans Knappertsbusch, 1888-1965. Second Edition.

2008: 978-1-901395-23-5: Philips Minigroove: Second Extended Version of the European Discography.

2009: 978-1-901395--24-2: American Classics: The Discographies of Leonard Bernstein and Eugene Ormandy.

Discography by Stephen J. Pettitt, edited by John Hunt:

1987: 978-1-906857-16-5: Philharmonia Orchestra: Complete Discography 1945-1987

Available from: Travis & Emery at 17 Cecil Court, London, UK. (+44) 20 7 240 2129. email on sales@travis-and-emery.com .

Lightning Source UK Ltd.
Milton Keynes UK
UKOW01f0817070717

304791UK00006B/170/P